WARD

Night Rider

And Other True Game Warden Adventures

by Terry Hodges

PRAISE FOR TERRY HODGES

"I once had hopes of becoming a game warden, but it wasn't to be. I have learned, however, that reading game warden stories by Terry Hodges is the next best thing. Terry's are the only outdoor books that I read in their entirety. His latest is an extraordinary piece of work."

—Tom Stienstra, San Francisco Examiner

"Not even in your imagination could you conjure up the intriguing stories in Terry Hodges' latest book. Most people have no idea how dangerous and complex a warden's job is, but they will, when they read this book. It's hard to put down without saying to yourself, One more story, just one more story."

—Bob Simms, KFBK Radio, Sacramento

"Lieutenant Terry Hodges is to wildlife protectors what Joseph Wambaugh is to big-city cops. ...evocative story-telling."

—Paul Dean, Los Angeles Times

"...great true stories by this celebrated and very talented California conservation officer and outdoor writer, and they have become required reading for fish and game cops across North America. He portrays game poachers and violators for what they are – thieves who steal fish, fur and game from everyone. This is a great read, and one every law officer and sportsman should read."

—Dave Richey, Outdoor Writer, The Detroit News

"The entire *Warden Force* series is a testament to the dedicated, hard-working game wardens not only in California but across the nation. Most people never see these men and women or even consider them. But they put their lives on the line every day to protect and preserve our natural resources. The "Warden Force" books are well written and highly entertaining. If you enjoy true adventures, humor, and the outdoors you will certainly enjoy these books. "

— Ron

"Terry Hodges has received national and state writing awards. Having read this book, I can certainly understand why. He is definitely a gifted and talented writer and storyteller. If you enjoy reading about the outdoors, wildlife or law enforcement, this book and probably the whole series should be at the top of your must-read list. Well done, Terry Hodges! I would give this book 10 stars if Amazon would let me. "

— William McPeck

"This is a great collection of stories. As an avid outdoorsman, I enjoy reading these as they are relatable to anyone that enjoys hunting and/or fishing. Each story gives enough detail so that you don't feel like something is missing but not so much that it becomes tiresome and drawn out. The length of each story seems to be just right for people like myself (kids, full time job, weekend warrior) who are busy, yet love to read engaging stories."

— Michael Shaffer

"Just when you think that something more bizarre can't occur, the next story doesn't disappoint with another amazing tale of wildlife law enforcement escapades."

— Kent

"Hodges is a gifted writer able to let you imagine you are right there experiencing the workings of California's game wardens. I have read most of his books and thoroughly enjoy his writing. He is able to capture factual events mixed with creativity to describe events in a manner that puts you there. Anyone who enjoys the outdoors will appreciate this book. "

— John Johnson

"I'm not a hunter, hiker, or a fisherman. I'm a life-long city kid, but I'm hooked. I love the underlying simplicity of identifiable good guys and bad guys, but what really hooked me is the author's ability to make me feel like I'm in the middle of situations I never even nearly experienced. I find myself wondering with the game wardens over how to set a trap for the bad guys and then eagerly reading the ensuing action, sharing the anticipation of success. Many of the stories end with an unanticipated twist, always resulting in a smile of satisfaction. Can't beat these stories for easy reading, education, suspense, and enjoyment."

— Amazon Reviewer

"We have every one of Terry's books save this one. Can't wait for it to arrive. Terry has developed a mastery in storytelling. You are there. When he discusses being out in the middle of the night, I feel like reading under the blanket with a flashlight. Truly. The easy read is perfection as well as understandable, but have to force myself to put it down as I don't want it to end so quickly. You'll better understand what wardens have to do other than check fishing licenses."

— Bill Adelman

"I always look for the "surprise" in a book that makes it great. Terry Hodges understands how to use surprise as an element of a good story and getting to wisdom. The preface points out three surprises often drawn from Hodges' game warden accounts: 'California has more natural diversity of wildlife and wildlife habitat than any other state'—and many of its own citizens do not yet realize that this is a rural state; it is not mainly urban. And some of the most depraved crimes are committed in the rural areas—it is not our urban centers which are the 'high crime' areas.

A second misconception which covers a surprise is that game wardens and conservation officers "are at greater risk of being assaulted and killed in the line of duty" than almost any other profession. Whatever else we think of the predators and abusers among us, this book documents the fact that we also harbor and pay great heroes who protect our most precious assets.

These stories enable us to stand beside our heroes who protect our habitats. Our heroes still exist. We join in appreciating them and for doing what they do—combatting the high crimes against Nature committed by some very ignorant, depraved, and well-armed human beings. Our wardens are heroes. Readers can join those who have received, and will receive, California's highest honor, the Medal of Valor. "

— **Tom Key**

WARDEN FORCE

NIGHT RIDER

and Other True Game Warden Adventures

TERRY HODGES

California Department of Fish and Game, Retired

Season 1: Episodes 1-13

v1.5

NOTE TO READER

This is not a novel. This book, like the other eight books of the WARDEN FORCE series, is a collection of short stories, all true, the fascinating and often harrowing experiences of real game wardens pursuing armed violators in wild and remote places. TV shows such as WILD JUSTICE (National Geographic), NORTH WOODS LAW (Animal Planet) and LONE STAR LAW (Animal Planet) introduced the public to the real-life adventures of game wardens and conservation officers, a public hungry for more. And now, for readers, the WARDEN FORCE series provides the most exhaustive and comprehensive work in literature on this little known and often dangerous profession.

***

The stories in this book are true, presented with as much accuracy as memory and existing records permit. I have, however, changed many of the names to protect the privacy of those who have already paid the price for their misdeeds.

Terry Hodges

Acknowledgements

To cover designer Tatiana Villa for her artistic eye
and endless revisions.

To audiobook narrator, Patrick J. Hinchliffe who worked
tirelessly to bring these stories to life.

To publishing consultant, Brian Schwartz for his enthusiasm,
abundance of creative ideas, and expert guidance.

To Joe Graziano, former CFO of APPLE INC., whose friendship
has made a great difference in my life.

To Barbara Leitner, who edited the stories in this book. Barbara
has been my friend and unpaid editor for years. I've even tried to
pay her a time or two. Her response? "You couldn't afford me."

And finally, to all the readers who have taken time to post a re-
view or drop me a note of appreciation.

Terry Hodges

CONTENTS

PREFACE

It surprises many who read my stories to learn of the great diversity of challenges faced by California's Fish and Game wardens. This is probably due to the general misconception of many as to the true nature of this state—the perception that California is mainly urban when in fact the reverse is true. In truth, California has more natural diversity of wildlife and wildlife habitat than any other state and is second only to Alaska in its vast expanses of wilderness.

Readers are also surprised to discover how hazardous my profession can be. Out of necessity, wardens work alone much of the time, often at night, with absolutely no hope for timely backup should things go wrong. And things go wrong, somewhere in the state, with distressing regularity. The dangers of this work are best illustrated by rather grim FBI statistics which clearly show that game wardens and conservation officers in this country are at greater risk of being assaulted or killed in the line of duty than are most sheriff's deputies and police officers.

I mention these facts because I have become increasingly aware of the responsibility that accompanies my telling the stories of California's wardens. It's important to me to tell these stories accurately and to enlighten my readers as best I can as to what it really means to wear a badge and a gun in this state on behalf of wildlife.

With this in mind, I present the following true stories—the experiences of good wardens pursuing a highly challenging and dangerous profession.

The Midnight Ride of Bonnie and Clyde

Warden Art Lawrence, California Department of Fish and Game, sat glowering in his parked patrol truck, the darkness of the night exactly matching his mood. He would miss the action. He glared at the dimmed digital display of his radio, the only light in the otherwise blacked-out interior of the vehicle, intent on the excited voices of wardens elsewhere.

The pilot of a Fish and Game airplane, just after midnight, had spotted a deer poacher working a high-powered spotlight in mountainous eastern Tehama County. The pilot had vectored wardens to the area, but the poachers, upon seeing approaching headlights, had made a run for it.

"He's raisin' a lot of dust . . . I can't see the road," came the adrenaline-hyped voice of one warden, his siren clearly audible in the background.

"Then back off," said another. "It ain't worth gettin' killed over."

Lawrence cursed his luck. The chase was occurring a mere four miles to the south, just across the county line, but it was a good two hours away by mountain roads, much too far. He could only sit and listen in frustration.

Every bit as frustrated as Art Lawrence was Warden Don Jacobs, who sat in his *own* idle patrol truck on *another* mountain road not far from Lawrence. Like Lawrence, Jacob's attention was locked onto his radio. As the chase continued, it now appeared that a second warden unit was about to intercept the fleeing poachers from another direction, the whole operation being directed from the aircraft a couple thousand feet overhead.

"You should see his headlights any second," said the pilot, peering down as the vehicles rapidly converged.

"Okay, I've got him," said the second warden, braking to make a head-on stop.

There followed about two minutes of silence over the radio, a silence that wore heavily on Lawrence and Jacobs. Finally, one of the arresting wardens spoke up.

"We're code-four," he reported. "We've got two suspects, a spotlight, and a rifle!"

"Ten-four. Good work," said the pilot. "I guess that's it for us tonight. We're gettin' low on fuel."

Lawrence radioed Jacobs on another frequency. "I guess that's it for us too," he said. He then suggested that he and Jacobs make a cooperative patrol back to Burney. They had a good 45-minute drive ahead of them, and there was always the remote chance of encountering a spotlighter on their way home.

"If you stay about five minutes behind me, we may get lucky," said Lawrence. "If I run into anybody, I'll give 'em my brights and blow on by 'em. Then you can set up on 'em."

Jacobs agreed. Soon they met at an intersection, then Lawrence set out, followed five minutes later by Jacobs. They were both dead tired, simply going through the motions, each convinced that all chance for excitement on this night had passed them by.

They were both wrong.

There was nothing pretty about Clyde Harmon McPhee. Nor was there any beauty to be found in the person of his mother, Bonnie Nadine, a five-foot-ten, 250-pound brute of a woman. And yet each of them spent considerable time before a full-length mirror at Bonnie's little cabin near Shingle Town, Bonnie searching for subtle signs of spontaneous weight loss and McPhee practicing looking tough and admiring the tattooed art work on his bare arms and chest. And often, of late, McPhee used the mirror for another purpose.

"I wish you wouldn't do that in the house," said Bonnie one night, as she noticed her son again poised before the mirror. She knew well what was coming. McPhee stood, feet apart, arms dangling at his sides, his eyes fixed on his image in the mirror. Suddenly he swept his right hand back, jammed it into the hip pocket of his Levi's and jerked it out bearing a snub-nosed, .38 caliber "Chief's Special" revolver. He then slipped the weapon back into his pocket, collected himself and went through the maneuver again. Then again and again.

"They're gonna catch you with that thing and send you back to prison," said Bonnie in the same loud, irritating screech of a voice that had driven McPhee's father away a quarter-century earlier.

"I ain't *never* goin' back to prison, Mom. *Never!*"

Anyone seeing them together would have noticed a facial resemblance, but there was an odd disparity in their physical sizes. For Bonnie Nadine dwarfed her 25-year old son in virtually all dimensions. But McPhee wasn't exactly small. True enough, three years in a Mexican prison had whittled him down considerably, but a year in the weight rooms in San Quentin had done much to bring him back. He now stood a wiry-strong, evil-looking five-foot-eight, his jet-black hair and beard contrasting strangely with the jailhouse pallor of his skin. Often seen together in their mountain community, mother and son made an odd-looking couple. The few locals who knew them enjoyed referring to them as *Bonnie and Clyde*.

Bonnie's concern that her son might be returned to prison was well founded. But his possession of the gun would make little difference, for he was already a fugitive, having jumped parole six months earlier with most of an 18-year sentence hanging over his head. The truth of the matter was that any brush with the law now, for anything, would certainly result in him being sent back to prison for a long time. Well aware of this, he had gone to the hills and moved in with his mother, subsisting on her welfare checks and food stamps, and whatever game he could bring down with an old .22 rifle.

With so much at stake, Clyde McPhee had become a careful poacher, his mother a reluctant and highly nervous accomplice. He would not risk killing deer near their cabin for fear of being turned in by nearby neighbors, nor would he risk using a spotlight at night. He limited his kills to those he could make using only the headlights of his mother's aging sedan. And even then he took precautions. He insisted that he and his mother dress up to go poaching, so that they would not look like poachers.

"We wanna look like we're just out for a drive," he would say. And he made plans with his mother, conspiring to defeat any situation that might arise that could put him under close scrutiny of the law. These plans, in fact, included the killing of cops if necessary.

And so it was that later the same night Clyde McPhee, dressed neatly in slacks and a clean sweater, his hair slicked back, and Bonnie Nadine, in full makeup, jewelry, a dressy blouse, and her best pair of Spandex tights, set out in the old sedan in search of game. But deer, on this night, proved hard to find. Mother and son prowled the mountain roads of southeastern Shasta County for hours, with Bonnie at the wheel, seeing occasional eyes in the headlights, but nothing that would hold long enough for a shot. It wasn't until after midnight, near Hatchet Peak, that their luck changed.

"Stop, Mom," said McPhee. "Back up and shine your lights on that meadow." Bonnie did as directed, backing the big sedan around until it sat crosswise in the road, its bright beams illuminating an opening in the forest. And there, transfixed in the lights, stood a doe and two half-grown fawns. McPhee grabbed the rifle from under the front seat and leaned far out the window with it. Squinting down the barrel, he trained the sights on a point midway between the bright, reflecting eyes of the doe. His index finger tightened on the trigger.

"Hold it, Clyde," said his mother urgently, and McPhee looked up in time to see a vehicle wheeling around the bend toward them. He had just enough time to haul himself and the rifle back inside before they were bathed in the bright headlights. And at that instant, as the approaching vehicle braked to a stop, a bright red light appeared near its driver's door. McPhee did his best to stuff the rifle back under the seat and compose himself as a large figure bearing a flashlight approached.

"Remember the plan, Mom," whispered Clyde McPhee. "Remember the plan."

Warden Art Lawrence had been battling fatigue, fighting to keep his eyes open on the long drive home. But upon rounding a curve and finding a big sedan totally blocking the road, its headlights trained on deer in a meadow, all weariness vanished. As he braked to a stop facing the driver's side of the sedan, he had time only to hit the switch to his red light and reach for his radio microphone.

"I've got a spotlighter," was all that he said, then he grabbed his flashlight and stepped out into the night.

Warden Don Jacobs, still five minutes behind, was confused over Lawrence's call, not knowing whether to set up an ambush or come rushing on in. He called Lawrence for more information, but got no reply. He tried again. No answer. He then jammed the accelerator to the floor, sending gravel flying, as he sped away in Lawrence's direction.

Lawrence in the meantime was carefully approaching a man and a woman in the sedan, nervous to be walking through his own headlights. He held his flashlight high, in his left hand, his gun hand resting on the holstered butt of his big Magnum revolver. He had seen plenty to justify detaining these people and searching the vehicle for guns. For he had seen the man in the passenger seat hunch forward and down in the classic "furtive movement" of stuffing something under the seat.

And the behavior of the two suspects, *after* this furtive movement, had been plenty suspicious in itself. Upon finding themselves fixed in the headlights and red light of an arriving patrol vehicle, they had not looked at it, but had stared straight ahead through their windshield like robots, certainly abnormal behavior.

"State Game Warden!" shouted Lawrence as he moved to approach, from slightly behind, the large woman at the wheel. "Ma'am, would you turn off the engine please?" Bonnie Nadine complied. "Now, would you folks put your hands up on the dashboard where I can see 'em, please?" They complied, and Lawrence directed his flashlight beam inside for a quick look around. *Nobody in the back seat, no weapons in view.* But he was puzzled over the way the two suspects were dressed. They looked as though they had just come from church.

"What's the trouble, officer? We're just out for a drive," said Bonnie, in her best innocent-lady voice.

"Well, I'm wondering why you're stopped like this in the middle of the road," said Lawrence.

"We were just turning around to go home," she said.

Good answer, Lawrence thought. But he was still certain that they had been up to no good. "Do you have any guns in the car?" Lawrence asked, now directing the flashlight beam at the male suspect.

"No guns," said Clyde McPhee. "We're not lookin' to shoot anything."

"Okay, sir," said Lawrence. "Would you mind steppin' out, please, keeping your hands where I can see 'em?"

McPhee complied, and as he opened the door and moved his legs to exit the sedan, Lawrence spotted a rifle stock protruding slightly from under the seat.

"Now come around to this side, please," said Lawrence, watching the man's every move. Again the man complied, but there was something about him that made Lawrence *real* uneasy. And there was something about Lawrence that made *Clyde McPhee* real nervous, for Lawrence, at six-foot-four and 255 pounds, was one of the largest officers he had ever seen.

With the male suspect out in full view, Lawrence now asked the woman to come out, and while she was struggling from behind the wheel, Lawrence noted that she appeared considerably older than the man. "Are you two related?" he asked.

"I'm his mother," said Bonnie Nadine.

With both suspects now out of the sedan, Lawrence instructed them to remain where they were, and he slipped around the rear of their vehicle and approached the passenger door. Without taking his eyes off the suspects, he opened the door, reached under the front seat and withdrew the rifle. Standing again, he slipped back the bolt of the rifle and ejected a shiny .22 hollow point cartridge into his hand. Rifle and cartridge he now carried to his patrol vehicle. As he did so, the male suspect started walking toward him, and experience and instinct were now shouting urgent warnings in the warden's brain.

"Hold it, sir! Stand back where you were," said Lawrence, at a half-crouch now, his left hand raised and signaling *STOP*, his right hand on his gun butt. The man hesitated a moment, then moved back to stand sullenly with his mother.

Lawrence anxiously glanced up the road and was relieved to see Don Jacobs' headlights appear. Jacobs, traveling fast, braked hard and slid in next to Lawrence's pickup. Two sets of headlights now illuminated the suspects. Jacobs stepped out, and the two wardens held a quick conference in low voices.

"I really don't like the looks of this guy," said Lawrence. "Keep a good eye on him." He then filled Jacobs in on the stop, the loaded rifle and what little he knew about the suspects so far.

"A mother and son poaching team?" said Jacobs. *"That's* a new one!"

Lawrence asked Jacobs to cover him and watch the woman while he searched the man. They separated as they approached the suspects.

"Sir," said Lawrence, "Step over here, please. I have to give you a quick pat-down search for weapons." McPhee exchanged a quick look with his mother, then approached Lawrence near the front of the sedan. But at this point all cooperation on the part of McPhee ceased. When Lawrence instructed him to turn around and face away, McPhee turned a full circle to again face the warden. Lawrence again asked the man to turn around, and once more McPhee did a full circle. And so it went, with McPhee deliberately, but passively, resisting the warden's demands.

Lawrence had intended to be as soft as possible in dealing with the man, not wanting to manhandle the guy in front of his mother. And like many large wardens, Lawrence was concerned with being perceived by others as a "heavy." But it was now apparent that the soft approach was not going to work. So, in a new voice, low and heavy with menace, Lawrence ordered the man to turn around and lace his fingers behind his head. McPhee now instinctively complied. Lawrence then approached from behind and grabbed the man's hands, locking them together.

It was obvious to Lawrence that the man had been testing him, taking measure of him, and he fully expected the man to try something. For this he was ready. But for what happened next, he was totally unprepared.

Suddenly the woman began screaming and ripping at the buttons on her blouse. "He doesn't have a gun. Here, search me! Search me!" In seconds, she had stripped off her blouse and had begun peeling off the Spandex pants.

"Hey, *stop* that!" shouted Jacobs, horrified, "*Stop* that, ma'am!" But soon the Spandex pants were down at her ankles.

"Search me! Search me!" she shrieked, kicking off the pants and ripping at her underwear.

"*Stop* that, ma'am! *Stop* that!" yelled Jacobs.

It was at this point that Clyde McPhee made his move. Lawrence's attention had been successfully diverted, and McPhee suddenly spun away, breaking the warden's grasp. But Lawrence caught McPhee's sweater from behind, and the garment, stretching like a giant bungee, brought the man to a halt. McPhee then whirled to face the warden, digging with his right hand for the pistol in his hip pocket. But Lawrence was on him like an avalanche, driving him to the ground, crushing the wind out of him.

"I think he's got a gun!" shouted Jacobs, who in a glance had seen McPhee going for his pocket, an act screened from Lawrence's view. Jacobs was now in action, crouched defensively, struggling to prevent an eighth-of-a-ton of shrieking, near-naked woman from rushing to the aid of her son.

But Clyde McPhee, face down in the dirt, was in no condition to use his gun. "You screwed up, didn't you, partner!" growled Lawrence into the man's ear.

"Yeah . . . I . . . screwed up," gasped McPhee. Lawrence plucked the pistol from the man's pocket and slipped it into his own. He then wrenched the man's arms behind his back, drew his handcuffs and snapped them onto the tattooed wrists.

"You're kidding me," said the jailer. "She ripped her clothes off?" "That's right," said Lawrence. "Right there in the middle of the road. It was *not* a pretty sight!"

The jailer roared with laughter. "Did you bring *her* in too?"

"No," said Lawrence. "We left her there, rolling around in the dirt, screaming at the top of her lungs. But her clothes were there, and her car keys . . . she could get home."

"Well, Clyde Harmon McPhee is a good catch," said the jailer. "He was a heavy-duty drug smuggler, before the Mexicans caught him. He did some real hard time in a Mexican prison before his mother got him exchanged. Then he did some time here before he was paroled. This'll send him back for a long time."

Lawrence now joined Jacobs at the booking window, where another jailer was questioning McPhee, a jailer with a sense of humor.

"Are you on any medication?"

"No."

"Do you have any communicable diseases?"

"No."

"Have you ever done time in a Turkish prison?"

"No."

"Did you cry when Ol' Yeller died?"

"No."

"You didn't cry when Ol' Yeller died? You must *really* be tough. Even *I* cried when Ol' Yeller died."

And so it went.

It was dawn before the wardens finished their business at the Shasta County Jail, and by then the adrenaline they had been running on had worn off. They were left tired and hungry, feeling totally drained. Even the humor of the incident was wearing thin. In its place, a much darker emotion was creeping in, a sinister, ugly thing that lodged in the pits of their stomachs. For the reality of their experience was now upon them

McPhee, in his desperation, had hoped to kill them, and the plan he had devised with his mother had nearly worked. It was by only the narrowest of margins that the wardens had been spared a close, nasty exchange of gunfire that would have likely left somebody dead. It had indeed been a near thing.

To Art Lawrence, who never knew fear, a close call with a gun-wielding criminal was of little concern. To deal with it, it was *his* style to simply buy more life insurance. But for Don Jacobs, this harsh reminder of the tenuous nature of his existence would have a more lasting effect. And as he drove home that morning, with the sun rising over the Sierra Nevada, he took some quiet time to marvel over things he had long been taking for granted . . . like the wondrous pleasure of simply being alive.

Night Rider

Pig poacher Alvin Sartori, at the wheel of his rusted barge of a sedan, cruised slowly, lights out, along the meandering, asphalt ribbon that was Highway 25. Crammed into the vehicle with Sartori was a motley assortment of his pig-poaching friends, both human and canine. In all, 10 pairs of predatory eyes peered expectantly ahead, scanning the bare, moonlit hillsides and barley fields of southwest San Benito County. Sartori stopped often to glass with his binoculars for game.

It was an hour before midnight when they approached Lewis Creek Road. And as they passed the intersection, Sartori noted the single-room building known as Tully Hall, a couple hundred yards down the gravel road. Twenty miles south of King City and well over a mile from the nearest ranch house, Tully Hall, once a school, sat alone and all but abandoned, a monument to a different age. But old buildings were of no interest to Alvin Sartori, who quickly returned his attention to the road ahead. And at that moment, movement caught his eye at the edge of a field.

There were nine pigs in the small herd. Only seconds earlier they had crossed the highway, led by a 200-pound sow. They now fed at the edge of a freshly harvested barley field, rooting through the stubble and grunting contentedly.

At the sound of the approaching vehicle, the sow gave a warning snort and set off at a trot, leading the herd, mostly half-grown piglets, farther into the field.

When Sartori spotted the pigs, he gunned the engine, raced ahead and made a sliding turn into the barley field. As he wheeled to a stop he snapped on his headlights, bathing the departing pigs in bright light. The doors flew open and Sartori and another poacher leaped out with rifles, Sartori with a large-bore deer rifle and his friend with a .22 semi-automatic. And as Sartori threw the rifle to his shoulder and steadied on the nearest of the fleeing pigs, he was vaguely aware of Tully Hall, beyond the pigs, barely illuminated in the far reaches of the headlights.

Sartori squeezed the trigger and the rifle boomed.

———————

The green pickup sat nearly invisible in the moon-cast shadow of Tully Hall. But it was a bright enough night that an observer at close range could have easily made out on its doors the shield-shaped logo of the California Department of Fish and Game. Inside, in the driver's seat, Warden Paul Maurer, who only seconds earlier had been battling drowsiness, was now as wide awake as he had ever been in his life. Rookie warden Andy Cortez, on the passenger side, was likewise all eyes and ears.

The wardens had come to this remote stretch of Highway 25 with hopes of ambushing poachers rumored to be working there. Ranchers in the area had reported hearing dogs and shooting late at night. Maurer had concluded that it had to be pig poachers. And now, after three boring hours of waiting, the action the wardens had craved was suddenly upon them, far surpassing their expectations, for they now found themselves almost directly in the line of fire of a couple of wildly firing outlaws.

Pop, pop, pop, BOOM, pop, pop, BOOM, pop, pop, pop, BOOM ...

Warden Maurer, staying low, peering over the dashboard through his binoculars, could see the muzzle flashes of the two rifles which were firing almost directly *at* him. And he could see pigs, in full flight, scattering across the field. He noted that following each of three successive shots from the big-bore rifle, a running pig crumpled and went down. The .22 rifle, a poor choice of weaponry for shooting pigs at a distance, was having no apparent effect.

Now the barking and yipping of dogs and the shouting of men were added to the sounds of gunfire. And dogs and men were now visible, running in pursuit of the fleeing pigs.

"What should we do?" said Warden Cortez, looking to the veteran warden, Maurer.

"We'll sit tight for a bit . . . until they do what they're gonna do and get back to their car," said Maurer.

The driver of the now-empty sedan turned the vehicle around, drove back to the intersection and turned onto Lewis Creek Road. The wardens held their breath as the car crept past Tully Hall, continued another couple hundred yards and stopped.

"He probably wants to get clear of the highway in case a car comes by," whispered Maurer. Just then, there came the sound of savage, frantic barking from the far side of the field.

"They've got one bayed up over there," said Maurer.

Then came a new sound, a harsh squealing. Seconds later a man strode by, less than 30 yards from the wardens, bearing under one arm the source of the noise, a live, struggling, 40-pound piglet. It was still squealing when the man arrived at the sedan with it, but there the squealing abruptly ceased.

Other men now returned to the sedan dragging the pigs killed in the initial shooting. The bloodied carcasses were heaved into the trunk, then the men hurried back into the field.

Again came the violent baying of dogs facing a cornered hog, and the wardens could see men rushing to the spot. More shouts, some loud profanity, more squealing, then relative silence. A few seconds later Maurer, through his binoculars, could see two men, each with a hind leg, dragging a good-size pig toward the highway.

"They must have used a knife on *that* one," whispered Maurer, for the use of knives instead of guns had become something of a macho thing among outlaw pig hunters. Spears, in fact, were used by some.

The sedan was in motion again, lights out, and again it crept by Tully Hall. At the stop sign, it turned left down the highway to meet the men and dogs coming out of the far side of the field. Maurer started the pickup, hit the kill switches that disabled his backup and stop lights, then eased out onto Lewis Creek Road to follow the sedan. At the intersection he turned left on the highway and stopped where he had a clear view of the sedan a couple hundred yards ahead.

Men and dogs now swarmed around the car. The dome light gleamed and the trunk lid was popped open again. The wardens watched as the last pig was muscled into the trunk and the lid slammed shut. The outlaws then began stuffing their dogs and themselves into the passenger compartment.

So intent were the outlaws in their haste to get moving that they failed to see the dark shadow that was a green pickup gliding up from behind. The last outlaw had just clambered inside, his ankle just clearing the door sill, when they suddenly found themselves bathed in bright lights.

"WARDENS!" cried one of the men as a bright red light appeared among the white lights behind them.

Alvin Sartori reacted instinctively and stomped the gas pedal to the floor. But the old sedan, jammed as it was full of men, dogs and dead pigs, managed little more than a leisurely departure. With little effort, the patrol truck kept pace, its siren now screaming.

It wasn't a lengthy chase. Sartori, after only a half mile or so, realized the folly of risking further flight in his overloaded car. He looked frantically around, searching for some escape, somewhere to run, a place to hide. But there was none.

"We got no choice," he said to his companions.

The others, each clutching a dog or two, cursed bitterly then sat glowering in silence as Sartori braked to a stop on a wide shoulder and shut off the engine.

Maurer snapped off the siren as he pulled up behind them, then the two wardens stepped out. And while Andy Cortez covered him from the right, Maurer cautiously approached the sedan from the left.

"STATE GAME WARDENS," he shouted. "EVERYBODY STAY IN THE CAR AND KEEP YOUR HANDS UP WHERE WE CAN SEE 'EM."

He edged up to a side window, his flashlight held high in his left hand, his right hand resting on the butt of his holstered Magnum revolver. Directing his flashlight beam inside, he was amazed at the mass of dogs and humanity stuffed together, and he grimaced as a strong odor washed over him, a powerful acrid mixture of hog smell, dog smell and the stench of unwashed human bodies.

"Sir," he said, addressing the driver. "I want you to step out slowly and bring the keys with you. The rest of you stay where you are." As the driver emerged, Maurer recognized him.

"Hello, Al," he said to his old adversary, a man whom he and many others in law enforcement considered to be the most dangerous man in the county. Sartori answered with a grim nod, and after noting the presence of a second warden, his eyes locked onto Maurer's. Sartori, a slim but deadly-looking criminal-type, had in the past killed at least two men that Maurer was aware of, simply gunned them down. There had been no witnesses to either shooting, and in both cases he had pled self-defense. Juries in both cases had failed to convict him.

"Turn around, Al," said Maurer. "Do you have any guns, knives or bazookas on you?" Maurer, prepared for anything, did a quick but cautious pat-down search of the man and directed him to stand behind the sedan, in the patrol truck's headlights.

Warden Cortez didn't know Sartori, but he could sense from Maurer's demeanor, despite the levity of the warden's words, that they were dealing with an extremely dangerous individual. Cortez's right hand crept back to his sidearm and unsnapped the safety strap. But even during the midst of this tense situation, Cortez could not help but admire, again, Maurer's impressive command presence. Maurer, he decided, at six-foot-two, with a magnificent walrus mustache and sharp, piercing eyes, would have made a great Wyatt Earp for the movies.

Maurer removed another outlaw from the car, then another, searching each, until only dogs of various breeds and sizes remained inside. Five sullen-looking pig poachers now stood squinting in the patrol vehicle's headlights.

Maurer next herded the five poachers closer to the grill of the patrol truck so that he could safely approach the trunk of the sedan. Cortez automatically moved back and off to one side so that he could better cover the five men. Maurer slipped the key into the lock and popped the trunk lid open. As he had expected, it was stuffed totally full of dead hogs, five in all. Three had been killed by bullets, one medium-size boar had its throat slashed, and one, a 40-pound piglet, had been killed by a swift blow with a claw hammer. The bloodied tool lay beside the warm carcass.

"Quite a night's work," said Maurer, turning to face Sartori. The man just shrugged.

During a quick search of the sedan, Maurer found a wicked-looking little sawed-off shotgun under the front seat. A single shot weapon of .410 caliber, missing most of its stock and all but a few inches of its barrel, it was loaded with a single .41 Magnum pistol cartridge. *A pig killer*, Maurer decided.

Maurer would have chosen to book Sartori for possession of the illegal shotgun, but with no room in the pickup for an additional passenger, the warden had to content himself with citing and releasing the man with his friends.

Four of the five outlaws helped Cortez load the five pigs into the patrol truck while Maurer stood back to cover Cortez. It was Sartori who stood idle, refusing to help with the work, and during the time it took the others to transfer the five pigs, Sartori's eyes never left Maurer. And Maurer knew then, with absolute certainty, that he and Sartori would tangle again, perhaps under circumstances with odds more to Sartori's liking.

It was well past midnight by the time the wardens concluded their business with Sartori and company and sent them on their way.

"Five poachers, five dogs and five pigs," said Maurer to Cortez. "Not bad!" Then he remembered the look in Sartori's eyes and felt a tiny chill run up his spine.

Months passed. And while Warden Maurer had no contact with Al Sartori during this time, he always knew that it would happen sooner or later. In truth, it was not only Al who was a worry to the wardens, but his father and four brothers as well—infamous poachers and criminals, all of them—violent, dangerous men. Fishermen and hunters up and down the Monterey County coast knew well of the Sartoris, and most were terrified of them.

But Warden Paul Maurer was a hard man to scare. He was what game wardens referred to as a "night rider," one not intimidated by darkness or by the very real and multiplied dangers of working alone at night. Outlaws in his part of the state had learned that even on the darkest of nights and in the most remote and menacing corners of his patrol district, he could show up at any time.

And so it happened one winter night, when Alvin Sartori, his brother Frankie and two others were struck with a craving for wild pork. The four of them, plus their pig dogs—two stout pit bulls and a giant Rhodesian ridgeback—piled into a pickup and headed out.

It was long after midnight, on another lonely stretch of Highway 25, about 35 miles south of Hollister, when they spotted pigs in a field along a creek. Alvin, the driver, pulled over just long enough for his brother, Frankie, to jump out with the dogs. He then drove slowly south again, having reasoned that it was a bad idea to leave the pickup sitting along the road longer than necessary. Only seconds later, headlights appeared, coming in his direction from the south. As the vehicle passed them, travelling at highway speed, all three men strained to get a look at it.

"What'd it look like to you?" said Al, watching the diminishing taillights in his rear view mirror.

"It was a pickup . . . just one guy, I think," said one of the others, peering back through the rear window. "But it never slowed down."

When the taillights had vanished, Alvin Sartori swung the pickup around, killed his headlights and headed north again. There was just enough moon to drive by, and as he crept along he reasoned that if the mystery vehicle meant trouble, he would soon know it. But he covered the half mile or so back to the field where he had left Frankie and the dogs without seeing anything of concern. He again turned his mind to the hunt.

As he expected, he heard the wild barking of dogs with a pig at bay when he and his friends jumped from the pickup. They raced across the field toward the commotion. The pig, a fierce-looking European-strain boar of about 260 pounds, stood with his back to heavy brush, hackles raised, and popping his jaws with rage. The dogs snarled and lunged and snapped at him from three sides, and every few seconds the boar charged one of them, slashing with ivory tusks that gleamed in the moonlight. One of the pit bulls, not quite quick enough, bore a four-inch gash on its flank.

"He's a mean one!" shouted Frankie above the din.

"Hold your light on him," shouted Alvin, drawing his pistol. Still nervous about the mystery vehicle and anxious to get out of the area, he wasted no time. He took aim between the two angry porcine eyes and pulled the trigger.

Warden Paul Maurer, heading home from a fruitless patrol, knew instantly he was on to something when he passed the slow-moving white pickup. It could have been a drunk returning from town, but somehow the warden knew otherwise. Without altering speed he continued on through a couple of turns, then killed his lights and headed back. He stopped at one end of a gentle, mile-long curve on which he should have seen the taillights of the white pickup. But there were none. Raising his binoculars, he glassed the road and immediately spotted the pickup, lights out, headed slowly in his direction. He was about to turn around again, to put distance between himself and the other pickup, when the vehicle stopped. Maurer then eased the patrol vehicle into the shadow of a cut bank and turned off the engine.

In the sudden relative silence, he immediately heard dogs fighting a pig. Less than a minute later he heard two distinct pistol shots. Again using binoculars, he spotted several men and dogs returning to the pickup. The men apparently tied the dogs in the vehicle, then two of them headed back across the field and disappeared into heavy brush. Then, as Maurer expected, they appeared again, dragging a large hog. And as they neared the road they actually picked it up and ran with it, heaving it into the back of the pickup. They then clambered in, the headlights flashed on, and they headed in Maurer's direction.

Maurer fired his engine and waited for the right moment as the pickup approached. Then he snapped on all his lights, including the red one, swerved into the oncoming lane and attempted a head-on stop. But the white pickup swerved to the right, causing Maurer to turn left to block it. Then it swerved sharply to the left to pass behind the patrol vehicle. Maurer, in his haste, missed reverse, and the vehicle careened around him and was gone. But Maurer was soon running code-three in pursuit.

Alvin Sartori, again finding himself pursued by Fish and Game, drew the stolen revolver from his belt and hurled it out the window into the forest. Next, he considered the patrol vehicle, whose lights were drawing closer in his mirror, and decided it made no sense to continue to run. He would take his chances face to face with the warden. He therefore put on the brakes and stopped.

Warden Maurer, upon rounding a bend, found the white pickup stopped in his path and had to brake hard to stop a vehicle length behind it. And there, in the back of the pickup, sitting with his back to the cab and holding a rifle at port arms, Maurer recognized Frankie Sartori. Maurer cautiously slipped out the door, intending to order Frankie to lay down the rifle, but at that moment the driver's door flew open and Alvin Sartori leaped out and did, perhaps, the singularly most stupid thing of his life. He charged directly at Maurer. The warden automatically drew his pistol and brought it to bear on the fast approaching outlaw, and in the two seconds that followed, a variety of things happened:

Knowing full well that he would not survive a fight with two or more of the murderous Sartori brothers, and aware that his life was in extreme danger, Maurer began his trigger pull. The hammer started back and the cylinder turned, aligning a shiny new hollow-pointed .357 Magnum cartridge with the pistol barrel, which, in turn, was aligned with the center of Alvin Sartori's chest. Simultaneously, Maurer was vaguely aware of Frankie Sartori shouting, "He's got his gun out!" By then, Alvin Sartori had covered half the distance to Maurer, and Maurer had pulled the trigger to a point where a strong breeze would have sent the hammer and firing pin slamming home. But at that last millisecond, Maurer stayed his pull, his brain having detected a change in the threat from Sartori. Was the man trying to stop? Sure enough, at that instant Sartori put on the brakes and slid to a stop a mere five feet from Maurer.

They stood frozen there for a moment, Sartori at a half-crouch staring at Maurer, and Maurer peering at Sartori over the sights of the revolver, each man suddenly struck by the immensity of what had nearly occurred. Then Maurer spoke.

"Get down on your stomach, Al," he ordered. But Sartori didn't respond. Maurer then raised the pistol higher, pointing the weapon directly at the man's face.

"GET DOWN ON YOUR STOMACH!" Maurer repeated, and there was such incredible menace in his voice and such a lethal look in his eyes that Sartori, for perhaps the first time in his life, experienced genuine fear of another human being. He immediately plopped down onto his belly.

"Now you," said Maurer, bringing the pistol to bear on Frankie Sartori, who still sat in the pickup bed, still holding a rifle, and was obviously considering his odds of surviving a shootout with Maurer. "Put the rifle down and climb out of there," said Maurer.

Frankie reluctantly complied, and soon joined his brother, face down in the dirt.

"YOU MEN IN THE TRUCK . . . STAY WHERE YOU ARE AND DON'T MOVE."

Maurer then eased back to the open door of his pickup, grabbed his radio mike and called San Benito County Sheriff's Office for a backup.

"We don't have a graveyard shift on duty," the dispatcher explained. "I'll have to get somebody out of bed." "Well, you better get *somebody*," said Maurer, "because I've got four men here at gunpoint."

Maurer now approached Alvin Sartori, who lay facing away from him in the dirt, and holstered his pistol. Reaching down, he grabbed the man's wrist and applied a twist lock.

"Al," he said quietly, "if you so much as twitch, I'm gonna hurt you *real* bad." He then wrenched the man's hands behind his back and applied the handcuffs.

He repeated the process with Frankie, using a second pair of cuffs he carried on his belt. Then, using a third set of steel handcuffs and some nylon flex cuffs he kept in his pickup, he handcuffed and searched, one at a time, the two men remaining in the cab of the white pickup.

Now he could relax, somewhat. But facing a half-hour wait for a backup officer, and with the trussed outlaws beginning to grow restless, he chose further action. He pulled the proned Sartori brothers to their feet and bound all four men together, connecting them elbow to elbow, using more of the nylon flex cuffs.

When the backup unit finally arrived, a full half hour later—they had sent a Hollister city cop—Maurer was examining a .222 cartridge he had removed from the chamber of Frankie Sartori's rifle. The arriving officer stepped out and duly noted the rifle and the four handcuffed outlaws. He then took a closer look at the outlaws and recognized the two Sartori brothers.

The officer stood there a moment, puzzled, looking around as though expecting to see someone else. He then approached Maurer and said, "You're by yourself?"

"That's right," said Maurer. The officer smiled, shaking his head in wonder and said with total conviction, "You guys are crazy!"

Later, when the officer had departed with the outlaws—three in the cage, and the fourth seatbelted securely in the front—Maurer walked over to his patrol truck which now contained the carcass of the slain hog. He stared at the animal for a short time, pondering its death that night by gunfire. Then he peered up at the moon, which seemed cold and not at all friendly. And as he climbed into his truck for the drive back to town, he reflected on the police officer's words. *You guys are crazy,* the man had said.

And Warden Paul Maurer concluded then, all things considered, that the man was pretty close to right.

DECISIONS

Wind, waves and utter darkness. Skipper Sam Randazzo, age 73, clenched his teeth and ignored the knot of nervous tension that grew like a boil in the pit of his stomach. Beneath his feet the old 55-foot purse seiner, *Nona Maria*, bucked and plunged like a rodeo bull.

It was a dangerous night for fishing. But among commercial fishermen, fair-weather sailors soon face financial ruin, a fact Randazzo was well aware of as he considered his options. Should he play it safe and seek shelter at Catalina Harbor, or should he go for the profits, take the calculated risk and make a set. Decisions. It seemed to Randazzo that his whole adult life had been one tough decision after another, brutal, gut-wrenching choices that could easily mean the difference between life and death.

For the hundredth time that night he glanced nervously at the radar set. Catalina Island, invisible in the darkness, appeared as a ghostly green mass on the screen, her jagged shore a mere quarter mile to the north. But Randazzo knew that a trap of barely submerged rocks lay much closer than that. "Jesus rocks," the fishermen called them.

He now turned to the sonar. A solid bottom 150 feet below printed clearly on the screen. But just above the bottom he detected something less distinct, irregular-shaped clouds of tiny signals. To Sam Randazzo these clouds held no mystery. He knew them to be alive, and to him they meant money. Reaching to a control panel, he snapped on a heavy switch and night suddenly became day. A million lumens of electric light burned into the choppy sea, and 150 feet below, a million tiny pairs of eyes took note.

Turning again to the sonar, Randazzo watched as the living clouds of signals began to rise, the multitudes of pencil-length, tentacled bodies responding to the light. For squid are nighttime spawners, their reproductive behavior triggered by moonlight. They are drawn to moonlight, ever upward, to the shallow water near the surface where they wheel and turn and clasp, a silent ballet in the moonlight.

But men like Randazzo had learned that squid were easily fooled, that powerful halogen lights could attract them and draw them like moths to giant flames.

Within minutes of the appearance of *Nona Maria*'s lights, the water beneath her hull was teeming with squid. Randazzo studied the school, calculating, weighing opportunity against hazard, then made his decision.

"Let her go," he shouted, and a crewmember with a sledgehammer struck the clasp of a pelican hook which sprang open, releasing the heavy 18-foot wooden skiff. The skiff, diesel-powered and manned by another nervous, rain-slickered crewman, slid backward over the sloping transom of the *Nona Maria* and splashed into the sea. The engine fired instantly, and immediately, as the *Nona Maria* went one way, the skiff moved off in the other, bearing the cable that was one end of the huge purse seine. Working together, while the *Nona Maria*'s lights still blazed and the net paid off her stern, the two craft moved to encircle the enormous school of squid.

Upon meeting at the far end of a circle of net that contained nearly the area of a football field, the skiff man passed his end of the net cable to a crewman on the *Nona Maria*. At this point, the circle of net hung vertically from the line of floats along its top. But aboard the *Nona Maria*, the crew now began winching in the slip cable on the bottom of the net, pursing it together beneath the school of squid. Soon the purse was complete, and the trapped squid were doomed.

As crewmen winched in the net and the entrapped squid became concentrated, Randazzo made a quick, but vital estimate. Could he handle a catch of this size? He knew that while alive, the squid would swim and remain at neutral buoyancy and weigh nothing in the net. But he also knew that as the squid were crowded ever closer together as the net was pulled in, a combination of stress and oxygen depletion in the water would kill them. As they died, they would become dead weight in the net—tons of dead weight. There could be real danger under such circumstances, for more than one purse seiner had been lost in this way, dragged under, stern first, before their frantic crews could slash the nets to dump an overlarge catch.

But on this night, Randazzo's catch was manageable, even under the existing poor conditions. He therefore shouted the orders that activated the brail—a large, winch-driven dip net suspended from a boom. The brail would transfer squid from the net to the seiner's hold.

Randazzo noted, at that time, that the squid were beginning to color, a curious phenomenon that occurred when they were highly stressed and short of oxygen. It was as though they would flush red with stress, turning from their normal ivory color to increasingly darker shades of pink. But upon dying, they would fade again to ivory.

Time after time the brailer dipped into the massed squid and lifted them, several hundred dripping pounds at a time, and swung them to the *Nona Maria's* waiting hold. And with each scoop, the *Nona Maria* settled a fraction of an inch deeper into the swells.

Randazzo looked on uneasily, worried over the fumbling performance of his six-man crew. Only two of them were old hands and experienced. The others, who included his own nephew, were green. And two of *those*, freshly arrived from Mexico, had only rudimentary knowledge of English, and both were fighting losing battles with sea sickness. The crew had yet to be welded into an effective team, and they were slow in responding to Randazzo's commands. Despite the chill wind, Randazzo sweated freely.

But despite Randazzo's fears, his crew, toiling on the rolling deck in their spray-drenched yellow rain gear, managed to labor both the catch and the net aboard without mishap. There now remained only the worrisome task of winching the skiff aboard, which was no mean feat in heavy weather.

Ramon "Gordo" Ochoa, Randazzo's portly, but most experienced, deckhand, caught the line thrown by the skiff man, pulled in the heavy wire-rope painter attached low on the skiff's bow and snapped the winch cable onto it. As he worked, Gordo sucked great draughts of damp air through the permanent stoma beneath his Adam's apple. His trachea had been lost to disease several years earlier. The *Nona Maria*'s engineer now applied power to the winch. As the cable came taut, the skiff thumped soundly against the *Nona Maria*'s sloped transom and began its climb up and onto the sodden pile of net on the main deck.

Along the *Nona Maria*'s transom were steel guides intended to keep the heavy skiff centered as it came aboard. And they would have worked on this night had the *Nona Maria* not taken a bad roll at a most inopportune time. The skiff, which was not yet secured on deck, was tossed out of the guides and slid left to jam against the *Nona Maria*'s port side. The *Nona Maria* immediately heeled heavily to port, and below, in her hold, 30 tons of dead squid began to flow like liquid concrete toward the port side. The *Nona Maria*'s already alarming port list increased steadily.

Randazzo bellowed orders as sea water poured in over the port side. The crew worked like demons, pushing and prying, trying desperately to muscle the skiff back into the sea. But it was securely jammed. Randazzo's fear now turned to panic, and he began shouting commands in Italian. The terrified Mexicans screamed back in Spanish.

But Gordo Ochoa stood silent on the tilting deck, knowing it was too late. He knew also, as sea water washed over his boots and as his right hand rose to touch the stoma beneath his throat, that he was very soon to be a *dead* man.

———

Aboard the Patrol Boat *Marlin,* Lt. Mark Caywood, California Department of Fish and Game, stood peering up at the night sky, judging the wind. It was 3:00 a.m., and the *Marlin* swung restlessly at her mooring in Avalon Bay, the light chop on the water in the little harbor an ominous sign. To go, or not to go—Caywood pondered the question.

It had been Caywood's intention to leave early on patrol and check squid boats for barracuda and white sea bass that the purse seiners were forbidden to keep. But the weather wasn't looking good. And because Avalon Bay lay on the north side of Catalina Island, the lee side under most conditions, it was difficult to judge from Avalon what the wind and sea would be doing along the south side of the island, where the squid fishermen would be working.

It would certainly be a marginal night at best, Caywood thought. But he also knew that he had made many of his most important arrests under marginal conditions, when the violators least expected him to be out and about. So, with this fact in mind, and with little more thought, he made what he would look back on as one of the more important decisions of his career.

"Let's go," said Caywood, addressing Warden Mike Darling, one of the *Marlin's* two boarding officers. Darling began securing equipment and making the *Marlin* ready for sea. Warden Jerry Karnow, the second boarding officer, had missed the patrol due to a court appearance on the mainland.

Caywood hit the starters on the *Marlin's* twin engines, and the big Detroit diesels roared to life. They surged rhythmically for a few minutes as they warmed, then settled to a steady throb. Mike Darling then took in the line from the mooring buoy, and they were underway.

The *Marlin*, 40 feet of wide-beamed aluminum hull, was not a pretty boat. She looked as though her builders had run out of funds and stopped construction five feet short of where her bow should have been. Her resulting blunt-nosed bow was not only unsightly, but a shortcoming sorely felt in choppy weather. Yet she was stout and plenty seaworthy, and with her flying bridge and her superb maneuverability she was a good platform for marine warden work. Caywood, a good mechanic and an excellent sailor, was an expert at getting the best out of her and regarded her with genuine affection.

Steering by the lights of the little town of Avalon, Caywood idled the *Marlin* through the nearly deserted harbor and past the casino, the famous old landmark on Casino Point. Then with nothing ahead but darkness and black ocean, Caywood turned to the radar set. Keeping the rocky shore well away to starboard, he started around the island.

Six miles later, as they approached the southeastern tip of the island, the *Marlin* came alive as the swells began to grow. By the time they rounded Church Rock, with the wind and sea full in their face, Caywood knew that there would be no boarding of squid boats on *this* night. Sheets of spray and green water broke over the *Marlin*'s blunt bow, and Caywood had to throttle back to ease the ride.

"We'll head on to Cat Harbor and hold up there until morning," said Caywood, his voice raised above wind and machinery. "Maybe the sea'll lay down a little by then." Darling's reply was lost in the darkness as they plowed and pounded along on an invisible ocean.

Twice they passed running lights of seiners on their way to port, then total darkness again. But a few minutes later a glow appeared a good ten miles ahead on the horizon, like the glow of lights from a town or small city. Recognizing it for what it was, Caywood altered course toward it.

"They're in Shark Cove, just beyond China Point," said Caywood, mainly to himself. "We'll just go take a quick look at them."

An hour later, the wardens could make out the lone seiner working close in to the treacherous shoreline. At a half a mile, Caywood made out the distinctive lines of the wooden-hulled, elderly *Nona Maria*.

"That's Sam Randazzo's boat," said Caywood, peering through binoculars. "They're getting ready to load their skiff."

Because the *Marlin* was approaching the seiner's port quarter, the wardens had a good view of the events that followed. Caywood saw the skiff jump its track as it came over the seiner's transom and he was instantly aware of her peril.

"Uh oh," said Caywood, "They just screwed up."

Caywood jammed the throttles forward, and the *Marlin* leaped ahead. He then grabbed the microphone to his marine radio.

"Coast Guard Radio Long Beach, this is Fish and Game Patrol Boat *Marlin*. I've got an emergency."

As the *Marlin* raced the last quarter mile to the distressed seiner, Caywood passed a hurried report to the Coast Guard. He then pulled alongside the *Nona Maria* and called out on the loud-hailer.

"SAM, WHAT CAN I DO TO HELP YOU?"

"THROW ME A LINE!" shouted Randazzo.

Caywood threw the engines into reverse and backed to within a few feet of the seiner's starboard side. At that moment, sea water reached the seiner's engine, which raced for a few seconds then died, a heavy white puff of smoke bursting from her stack. And with the death of the engine, the generator died, killing the huge halogen flood lights as well. Now only the *Marlin*'s floodlights illuminated the scene.

Darling was ready with the inch-and-a-quarter nylon towing line and tossed it across to Gordo, who received it with the enthusiasm of a condemned man freshly reprieved.

A more agile crewman then scrambled forward with the line, and acting on Randazzo's shouted order, secured it to *Nona Maria*'s mast. Randazzo, grasping at straws, was hoping to be pulled upright by the patrol boat.

But it was far too late. The seiner's port side was totally awash, and she was going down fast. Randazzo reluctantly faced this grim fact and ordered his crew to abandon ship. They hurriedly threw on life jackets, fumbled with fasteners, then one by one jumped into the sea. Hand over hand on the towline they began pulling themselves through the rough water toward the *Marlin*.

But the *Marlin* was now herself in peril. The huge net had floated free from the *Nona Maria*'s flooded stern and was spreading across the water. Caywood was forced to move the patrol boat about 70 feet from the sinking seiner. He simply could not risk fouling the *Marlin*'s screws in the net or other floating debris. With wind and sea driving them steadily toward the rocks, Caywood knew well that the survival of *all* of them, at this point, depended on his making no mistakes.

Aboard the *Nona Maria*, now barely afloat, yet another small crisis had arisen: Randazzo's nephew, the last member of the crew yet aboard, could not get his life jacket on. It was hopelessly knotted and tangled. Without hesitation, Randazzo tore off his own life jacket, strapped it onto his nephew and ordered the reluctant man over the side. Then Sam Randazzo, still strong despite his age and tough as Italian boot leather, took a last look at his boat, kicked off his boots and dove into the cold sea.

The wardens expected the old fisherman to drown, but to their surprise he swam the 70 feet or so to the waiting *Marlin*, actually reaching her before his crew. And he remained on the patrol boat's swim step, helping them, boosting them up the ladder as they arrived.

The two new Mexican crewmen tumbled aboard first, their teeth chattering like castanets. But the next man, frozen to inactivity by cold, fatigue and terror, clung to the ladder with a death grip, but could not climb. Seeing this, Caywood dashed from the controls, reached over the transom, grabbed the man by the back of his life jacket and somersaulted him aboard.

Next came Gordo. Exerting all his strength, Darling dragged him aboard, half drowned, leaving only Randazzo's nephew in the water. But the nephew had somehow lost his grip on the towline and was drifting away toward the rocks.

At about this time the *Nona Maria*, belching great bubbles of air and diesel fuel, rolled over and slipped beneath the waves. Caywood hurriedly untied his towline from the towing bit and passed it to Darling to attach a float buoy. But there wasn't time. The line was dragged from Darling's hands to snake over the side and disappear.

Caywood now assessed his situation anew: Wind and waves had driven them perilously close to shore, and Randazzo's nephew, for whatever reason, was unable to swim to the *Marlin*. The *Marlin* would have to go to him. But the man was dangerously close not only to a floating tangle of net and line, but to the first of a series of exposed rocks. To Caywood, however, the worry was not so much the *exposed* rocks, but the invisible ones just beneath the surface. The *Marlin* was now in real danger.

Decisions. Judging distance, calculating, glancing at the fathometer, Caywood hesitated but a moment. He then spun the *Marlin* around, dodged some debris and headed for Randazzo's nephew. Darling was ready with a ring buoy on a line and made a perfect toss to the man who grabbed and clung to it. Darling then pulled him in to the swim step and hauled him aboard. Caywood spun the *Marlin* again, this time gratefully heading her for deep water. But floating debris lay everywhere, dangerous stuff that could entangle the *Marlin*'s propellers and stop her dead in the water. And should this happen, within minutes the *Marlin* would die on the rocks along with everyone aboard.

Caywood chose a path through the wreckage and jammed the throttles full forward. The twin diesels roared and the *Marlin* raced ahead at full speed. Should a line now foul her props, perhaps momentum would carry her through. Caywood held his breath, expecting at any second the shudder and bumping and thumping that would herald disaster. But it never came. The *Marlin* plowed through it all and reached open water. Caywood could breathe again.

During the trip home, as dawn was breaking and Caywood steered the *Marlin* for Long Beach, Darling attended the rescued men. Gordo was in the worst shape, having miraculously hauled himself through the water using only one hand, the other being occupied in covering his stoma. He had nearly drowned, and Darling had been forced to lay him over the towing bit when he got aboard to drain him of seawater. He now lay on deck, bundled in blankets.

Darling got Randazzo and the others out of their wet clothes and into dry Fish and Game coveralls. With Fish and Game patches on both sleeves, these garments were the uniform in which the marine wardens often worked, and Darling couldn't help chuckling at the sight of such a bedraggled looking and unlikely bunch to be sporting Fish and Game colors.

Immediately following the *Nona Maria*'s demise, Caywood had radioed the Coast Guard. He had made his report, a brief account of the incident and resulting rescue. But others heard it too. Also hovering over marine radios and hanging on Caywood's every word were the skippers of seven purse seiners, each headed back to Long Beach with their catches. They would arrive well ahead of the *Marlin*.

Of these seven men, two had been arrested by Caywood, all had been hounded by him, and although they respected him, none of them had any reason to like him. And yet when the *Marlin* tied up at what had been *Nona Maria*'s berth at Long Beach, all seven skippers were there on the dock waiting.

"Hey, Mark," said one in his heavy Sicilian accent, "Come' ere, we wanna talk to ya." When Caywood approached them, the same man looked him in the eye and said, "We wanna thank ya! We know you'd do the same for us, and we'd do the same for you." Each man had then shaken his hand with genuine gratitude.

Two days later, a package arrived for Mark Caywood at the Long Beach office of Fish and Game. Upon opening it, Caywood found six neatly folded sets of warden coveralls. He then recalled Randazzo's words, "I'll get these back to you cleaned and pressed."

Like Mike Darling, Caywood had been amused at the ludicrous sight of Sam Randazzo dressed not only in a warden uniform, but one several sizes too large. And yet the image that would most vividly remain in Caywood's memory was that of Sam Randazzo shortly after being dragged aboard the *Marlin*. The old skipper had been the last one to come aboard, having insisted that his crew be rescued first.

He had remained on hands and knees on the deck for a while, dripping sea water, chest heaving, too cold and exhausted to rise. And he had peered up at Caywood, his old nemesis, the tireless enforcer of laws that he, Randazzo, detested and said, "I never thought I'd ever be happy to see Fish and Game."

Caywood had just grinned at him and replied, "We're from the government, Sam, we're here to help!"

A Second Second Chance

It lay in ambush in the shadow of the highway bridge, in the moss-green depths of Butte Creek. Nearly invisible in the dim light on the muddy bottom, it waited, its attention riveted to the slick surface above.

More a machine than a thinking animal, it was nonetheless a highly efficient predator—18 pounds of slippery-skinned muscle, fork-tailed, frog-faced and bewhiskered. And while channel catfish were never pretty, this one, to add to its naturally sinister appearance, bore an ugly scar on its back, just behind its spined dorsal fin, a poorly healed reminder of a near-fatal encounter years earlier with a great blue heron.

While most of its breed were at rest during the day, catfish being primarily night-feeders, this one was alert. For it had learned that springtime days meant opportunity at this spot. The reason was readily apparent overhead where hundreds of cliff swallows swooped and soared. They flitted about like bats, snatching insects from midair and returning often to their little mud-igloo nests which clung to every conceivable nook and corner of the underside of the bridge.

In one of these nests, as four partially fledged swallow chicks jostled for space, one was bumped out through the circular entrance. It tumbled 12 feet to the water below and landed with a tiny plop. And as it struggled on the surface, a dark shape rose beneath it. It was over in an instant. The surface suddenly erupted in a swirl of green water, and the chick was gone.

The big catfish glided back to its waiting place in the shadows. And there it lay until the sound of an approaching boat motor sent it retreating back beneath a cut bank.

Fish and Game Warden Fred Brown was in no particular hurry as he backed his patrol car to the open doors of his storage shed and hitched on the trailer bearing his outboard-powered aluminum boat. There was still better than an hour of daylight remaining, and the outlaws he planned to hunt would probably not venture out until after dark. So, he had plenty of time to ponder the information he had received a half-hour earlier at a gas station in town.

"They're usin' twig-lines on the river," the informant had told him. "They stopped here this morning with a washtub full of catfish."

Brown had carefully questioned the man further and was told that two men, personnel from a nearby military base, were running their illegal lines somewhere on the Feather River.

"How do you know they're doing it in the Feather?" Brown inquired.

"I asked 'em," the man replied.

Brown regarded this information with suspicion, for while it was common for outlaw fishermen to show off their illegal catches, they would rarely divulge the truth about where they fished.

When it came down to a decision that afternoon, when the warden left town, he ignored the route to the Feather River and opted instead to follow a hunch and head west for a little river that meandered south through the Sacramento Valley rice country.

Butte Creek, he thought. *It's got to be Butte Creek.*

The valley was aglow with the golden light of the approaching sunset when the warden neared the dense line of cottonwoods and willows that bordered Butte Creek. As he neared the bridge, he hit the brakes when a hen pheasant dashed across the road ahead. In close pursuit, a tiny mob of nine fuzzy chicks scurried after her, disappearing into the tall grass and cattails that bordered the road.

Two cars and a pickup were parked near the bridge as Brown drove across and turned downstream along Butte Creek's west bank. A key got him through a locked gate, then he continued a quarter mile farther to his hidden launching spot. Five minutes later, the boat was in the water and Brown was pulling on a pair of coveralls which hid his uniform. A battered blue ball cap completed the disguise, and with a pair of fishing rods and a tackle box in the boat, he looked like just another fisherman. He stepped in, shoved off, gave the outboard's starter cord a pull and was on his way.

The little outboard buzzed along as Brown headed upstream. And when the bridge came into view, he noticed two things in quick succession: First, he saw three men in a small boat beneath the bridge, and second, a man on a motorcycle was stopped on the bridge above, peering down at the three men. The men in the boat had ceased whatever it was they were up to when Brown's boat pulled into view, and as the warden drew near he saw one of the men in the boat put down a long metal pole he had been using a few seconds earlier, prodding the underside of the bridge.

Drawing nearer, Brown recognized the man on the motorcycle. It was Stanton Boggs, Gridley's chief of police. Boggs, in turn, had by then recognized Brown and was signaling to him, pointing downward and mouthing the words "down there." Brown nodded almost imperceptibly and continued on. He gave the three men a friendly wave as he passed them beneath the bridge, continuing upriver.

Brown motored on upstream until he was out of sight around the first bend, then he beached the boat. Stepping onto the bank, he slipped out of his coveralls, tossed his cap aside, grabbed his binoculars and headed back downstream on foot.

Sneaking through the willows, Brown was able to reach a point where he could train his binoculars on the three men in the boat. As he adjusted the focus, he noted that one of the men was operating a small outboard motor, holding the boat stationary against the current while the other two were engaged in puzzling activity: The one in the bow was shooting a pellet rifle while the one in the middle wielded a long-handled frog gig, and both appeared to be attacking swallow nests on the underside of the bridge. Brown immediately walked the remaining yards to the bridge, forced his way through the willows and called out.

"Hold it, men!" Three heads swiveled his way. "State Game Warden. What are you up to?"

Silence.

"Swallows are protected," Brown continued. "You can't disturb their nests."

Finally the man with the frog gig found his voice. "We weren't bothering 'em," he said. "We were just knocking down some of the old nests from last year."

"That's right," said the one with the pellet rifle. "Just the old ones."

"Well, you'd better find something else to do or you'll end up in trouble," said Brown.

They acknowledged, and the one handling the outboard swung the boat around and they headed downstream.

On his way back to his boat, Brown pondered the actions of the three men. *Why would grown men want to destroy swallow nests?* He had no answer.

Dusk found the warden slowly motoring upstream in his skiff, scrutinizing the riverbanks, his keen eyes searching for anything out of place. Twig lines could be difficult to spot, even in daylight, but in the fading light it took a trained eye. Occasionally he would work a likely spot with a long-handled gaff hook he had made for that purpose, groping into the depths, blindly searching.

It was nearly dark when he reached the One-Hundred Drain, a stream that flowed into Butte Creek from the east. While only 15 feet across, it was steep-banked and deep, like Butte Creek, and lined with willows. Brown paused for a moment, pondering a new decision. *Butte Creek, or the Drain?* he wondered. Again it was a hunch that guided his hand and sent the skiff nosing up the meandering One-Hundred Drain. And almost immediately he found the first line.

Movement caught his eye as a small, partially submerged willow limb had suddenly dipped an inch or two, causing a small disturbance on the surface. He went to the spot and passed his gaff beneath the limb. Hooked on the gaff when he drew it out was a single monofilament line. He pulled it in, hand over hand, bringing up a nice three-pound catfish.

Using his pocket knife, Brown quickly cut a tiny notch from one of the fish's fins, an identifying mark that could come in handy later. He then dropped the fish back into the water, still attached to the twig line.

Moving upstream again, Brown marveled at what an efficient poaching method twig-lining was. The small limbs to which the twig lines were attached acted like fishing rods, the resilience of which prevented a hooked catfish from getting a solid pull on the line to break free.

The warden had gone only a short distance farther upstream when he located line number two, and number three was not far beyond that. Neither line had yet hooked a fish, and both were baited with plump carp minnows. The warden now worked by the light of a small flashlight, the lens of which he had covered with black tape, all but a narrow slit. But a bright half-moon had begun to shake free of the ragged line of willows to the east, and visibility was beginning to improve.

While examining line number three, Brown heard an outboard start far upstream. Then it stopped. He knew then that it would be safe for him to go a bit farther and maybe locate more lines. His outboard was a quiet one, and at an idle it would be very difficult to hear from any distance. So, he continued on.

He found two more lines before rounding a bend and blundering onto a camp. There were sleeping bags, an ice chest and an unlit Coleman lantern visible in the moonlight. But fortunately there was nobody home. As he motored by, he noticed marks in the mud bank where a boat had been recently beached there.

He proceeded only a little farther where he found twig line number six. After marking another nice catfish on this line, he yielded to caution and turned around, heading downstream, careful to keep the outboard at an idle.

He passed the deserted camp and continued a hundred yards beyond it to a suitable spot where he dragged his boat from the water and stashed it behind some brush. He then grabbed a bag of gear and headed upstream on foot. He found the willow tree he was looking for, one he had spotted from the boat. It was old and bent, with one of its heavy limbs slanting out over the stream. Brown crawled out on the limb through a dense tangle of twigs and branches, breaking off those that barred his passage. Reaching the spot he was seeking, he cleared something of a nest for himself, six feet above the water. He found, to his satisfaction, that it afforded him a clear view of one of the twig lines, a mere 10 feet away.

Pleased with the spot, he backed down the limb onto the bank, and after laying out his big flashlight and his camera, he settled down to wait. He ignored the light dew on the grass and lay back, lacing his fingers behind his head, peering up at the moon. And as he breathed deeply, drinking in the damp, earthy smell of the marsh he had grown to love, he delighted again at his good fortune to be a game warden.

It was pushing 3:00 a.m. when the putter of an outboard brought him out of his thoughts. They were coming. He snatched up his camera and crawled out onto the limb, flattening his body against it, and as he peered out across the moonlit water he caught his first glimpse of the poachers. There were two of them, just as he had expected. They pulled out of sight for a few minutes as they apparently worked a line that was farther upstream. Then they headed straight for him. He felt his pulse quicken as they approached, and his stomach fluttering with the pre-encounter butterflies he knew so well. He steeled himself for anything from frowns to gunfire.

One man handled the motor as the other sat poised in the bow with a gaff hook. *They've done this before,* Brown thought, as the boat came gliding to within spitting distance. The bowman hooked the twig line in an instant, tossed the gaff aside and began pulling in the line. Brown chose this moment to aim his camera and squeeze the shutter release.

FLASH.

Both men jumped, the boat tipping dangerously. "What was that?" said one, peering wildly about. "I don't know," said the other, blinking in confusion. "Lightning maybe?"

Then Brown was astounded to see them shrug it off as some natural phenomenon and return to their work as though nothing had happened. Brown hurriedly prepared his camera for a second shot.

FLASH.

Knowing they would soon spot him, Brown followed the second photo with a shout. "STATE GAME WARDEN, MEN. YOU'RE UNDER ARREST!"

They nearly capsized.

The arrest went without a hitch. The two frightened poachers cooperated completely with Brown when he demanded that they show him all of their lines. They led him to a total of 14, including the ones that Brown had already found. And they had been well on their way toward filling a large tub with fish. Sorting through the tub, Brown located the two fish he had marked earlier.

A *good tight case,* thought Brown as he wrote out the citations, referring to information on the military identification cards that both men had produced. They were from a nearby military base. His hunch had paid off.

It was an hour before dawn when Warden Brown headed back down the One-Hundred Drain, anxious for a quick meal and some sleep. But he was about to find that his work for the night was not yet over.

As he reached the mouth of the One-Hundred Drain and was about to turn left into Butte Creek, he happened to look to his right. And there, to his surprise, was another boat. Without hesitation, he swung the skiff upstream, keeping the little outboard at its quietest idle. As he approached, he noticed that the boat, which was apparently anchored with its bow facing upstream, was moving slowly sideways across the creek with no visible means of propulsion. But as he drew nearer, he noticed a wet line reflecting in the moonlight, a line which emerged from the water on one side of the boat and apparently re-entered the water on the other side. And he could see that the occupants of the boat appeared to be pulling themselves slowly sideways with the line.

A *setline*, thought Brown. *It must run from bank to bank, clear across the river.*

There were three men in the boat, jabbering among themselves, their attention on the setline. But suddenly one of them waved the others silent and pointed in Brown's direction. Brown was ready and hit them with the bright beam of his flashlight.

"STATE GAME WARDEN! DON'T ANYBODY MOVE!"

The poachers sat frozen for a moment, but then the one in the bow, who sat facing aft with the exposed portion of the setline lying across his lap, suddenly came to life. He grasped the line with both hands, and despite Brown's shouted warning flung it over his head, behind his back. The line cleared the bow of the boat and sank from sight.

Brown, annoyed over the loss, at least temporarily, of his evidence, gunned the outboard and dashed up to the anchored boat with its three badly shaken occupants. And as he again illuminated them with his light, he recognized them as the three men he had encountered hours earlier under the bridge, the ones who had been harassing the swallows.

"Pull in your anchor, men, and follow me over to the bank," said Brown. "And keep your hands out where I can see 'em."

The man in the bow moved to comply, and as he pulled in the first eight feet of anchor rope, to his dismay and to Brown's delight, the setline again appeared. One of its many hooks had lodged securely in the anchor rope.

Brown quickly hooked the setline with his gaff, and as he began to pull part of it aboard he saw something that stopped him cold.

He stared horrified at the line for a moment, then turned to face the three suspects, anger welling up within him. For each of the hooks on the long setline—20 of them as it turned out—was baited with the tiny lifeless body of a baby swallow.

It was dawn by the time Warden Brown made it back to his patrol car, and after loading his boat on the trailer he paused to examine the evidence from his night's work. There were the catfish from the first case and the numerous coiled twig lines. There was a ten-foot frog gig and a pellet rifle freshly seized from the swallow killers, plus the heavy burlap sack containing the fish they had taken on their ill-baited setlines. As Brown gazed at the wet burlap sack, he detected movement within. Pulling the sack over to him he peered inside, and again he marveled at the monster catfish.

Pushing 20 *pounds*, he thought, and he tugged the big fish out of the sack. He wanted a look at it in the growing daylight. It was then that he noticed the twisted scar on its back.

"Looks like you had a bad brush with something," he muttered, running his finger over the old wound. There was still life in the old fish, for its gills were pulsing weakly as the warden slipped it back into the sack.

Too bad I can't release it, Brown thought sadly as he walked around to the driver's side of his patrol car. But it was important evidence in an important case. The swallow killers needed to pay dearly for their crimes, and their punishment needed to be a warning to others.

Brown slipped behind the wheel, started the engine and pulled away. But he had gone only a few yards when he suddenly hit the brakes and stopped. He threw open the door, slid out again and hurried back to the trailered boat. He pulled the wet sack over to him again, and again he pulled out the big fish. Slipping his hands beneath it, carefully avoiding its sharp spines, he gently picked it up and carried it to the water.

"Looks like you get a second second chance, big guy," he said as he gently laid it in the shallows. The big fish lay there awhile, the pulsing of its gills growing gradually stronger. Then, with a flip of its tail it was in motion. With another it gained deep water and was gone.

The Vision

There were no witnesses to Chong Sung's arrival in America. None, that is, but the harbor seals and what few sea birds that dared to brave the southwesterly gale that had battered the jagged coastline for two days running. And Chong Sung's was no gentle landfall. Driven shoreward by high winds, at a place not of his choosing, his boat was battered and wrecked on the rocks, and he found himself fighting for his life in the cold, angry sea.

He fully expected to die. But when death appeared imminent, he was snatched by a giant breaker, hurled past the rocks, and flung onto a narrow gravel beach. He lay there for a while, half-drowned, still clinging to wooden wreckage of the tiny craft that had miraculously borne him a third of the way around the world.

When at last able to stand, he searched among the rocks for signs of the others, his companions during the grueling six-month ordeal at sea. But there were none. Of the brave and hopeful young men who had sailed for America in the eight small fishing junks, it appeared that only he had survived.

Cold and shivering uncontrollably, he turned to the high cliffs that towered above the beach. A trail angled up the irregular face, a path worn by centuries of use by a people not all that distantly related to himself. He began the climb, his chilled limbs weakened by weeks of hunger.

Upon reaching the top, he glimpsed for the first time the gray-green hills of California, the Fusang of the ancient Chinese mariners, the Land of the Mountain of Gold. But his thoughts were not now of gold. Nor, perhaps, would they ever be again.

Why was I alone chosen to live?

Ignoring the cold and wet and hunger, Chong Sung turned and faced the sea and distant China. And then, at the edge of the cliff top, with the bitter wind full in his face, he knelt and prayed his thanks to his god.

A century and a half later, another man stood on this spot, on the cliff top overlooking the South Headlands of Caspar Bay.

It was a special day for Fish and Game Warden Mervin Hee, his first day of a dream come true. As on all special days of Mervin's life, he had felt compelled to visit this spot by the sea, a place of special significance to him, a place where he came to ponder the meaning of his life.

Perhaps it was because this place, above all others, brought the essence of his heritage into sharp focus. For it was here, in the fall of 1852, that his great-grandfather had struggled ashore, more dead than alive, after a sea voyage of epic proportions. It was the place where it had all begun.

As Mervin stood there, gazing out to sea, he thought back on his life, on what it meant to grow up as a member of the only Chinese-American family in the nearby town of Mendocino, to live where three generations of his family had been born and had spent their lives. And he pondered with bitterness the hardships his ancestors had experienced there, the hatred, the persecution that had driven other Chinese families to flee. But not Mervin's family. They alone had stood fast, and they alone had prevailed. In this, Mervin took grim pride. But he mourned the fact that his father, who had been born here and had lived and died here, had gone through his life never really feeling that he belonged, never really feeling American.

But Mervin Hee forced these painful thoughts aside, for he had not come to dwell on the past, but to celebrate the present.

I did it, Grandfather! I made it happen.

As the first sunlight of the new day bathed Caspar Bay in golden light, Mervin's thoughts turned again to a brief moment in time, a moment of inspiration that had occurred, it seemed, a lifetime ago. He coaxed the memory into sharp focus, as he had a thousand times before. And he could see it all, clearly, the forested canyon, the rutted dirt road, the sparkling waters of Two Log Creek.

He could see the old pickup truck grinding along, his brother and brother-in-law in front, and himself as a boy of 12 years old riding in back. They had been returning from a deer hunt when it happened, when the thought first struck him, the thought that had become a dream that had become an obsession. He recalled the instant it had occurred, the exact moment of decision as the old pickup was churning through the shallow waters of the ford across Two Log Creek.

I want to be a game warden! I want to be the game warden here in Mendocino County and drive my patrol truck across Two Log Creek!

Months earlier, he had watched a warden drive a Fish and Game truck across the creek, and now he imagined *himself* in the green patrol truck, the badge on his chest, the shield-shaped, blue and gold patches on his khaki sleeves, the emblem with the prowling golden bear. And he could picture himself so clearly, driving his truck across the creek.

But unlike the *wanna be* dreams of other young boys, Mervin's dream didn't fade. It grew stronger over the years. By the time he entered high school, he had a plan and knew exactly what he wanted to do with his life, and he had correctly concluded that his father was right—education would be the key to his success. So he worked hard at his studies, ever mindful of his goal.

By the time he enrolled in college, he knew what he was up against, of the staggering odds against his succeeding. He knew by then that there were literally thousands of applicants for the dozen or so game warden positions available each year. But he clung to his dream. And when doubt crept into his thinking, he would summon the vision of himself in the green patrol vehicle plowing through the waters of Two Log Creek, and the vision would restore his resolve.

Even with the Bachelor of Science degree in hand, when the grueling years of studies and exams were behind him, he remained light-years from his goal. While well qualified now to take the warden's exam, he had found, to his dismay, that the exam was given only once every two years, and he had over a year to wait for the next one.

But he had to work, so he took a job with the Department of Parks and Recreation. He became a park ranger at the Salton Sea, where, as luck would have it, he enforced mainly Fish and Game laws. He impressed everyone, including local Fish and Game wardens, with his hard work and keen instincts for law enforcement work. And several months later when the warden's exam was finally given, he was waiting at the door.

Nobody was surprised when Mervin did well on the exam, and yet a good score didn't guarantee a job. But at least he was now on the hiring list and infinitely closer to his dream. There was nothing now but to wait. Weeks passed. Months passed. A year passed. Then at last, nearly two years after the warden's exam, Mervin was offered a warden's position in San Joaquin County. He accepted the job immediately, giving hardly a thought to the $300 a month cut in pay he would experience. His jubilation was beyond words, and on one very special day in the summer of 1979, he was sworn in.

A few days following his hiring, Mervin visited Mendocino, the little town that would forever be home to him. It was as it always was, a cluster of stately Victorian homes built on a high peninsula jutting out into the sea. And as always, in sharp contrast to the conservatively painted Victorians, stood the ancient wooden joss house, a Chinese temple, painted red with green trim. Mervin winced when he saw it, as he always did after an absence, for it had been, throughout his life, a stark reminder that he and his family were somehow different from other residents of Mendocino, somehow considered foreigners despite over 140 years of continuous habitation here.

The joss house was an elevated structure accessed by a tall, wide stairway, and above its front door was a large plaque bearing three symbols in Chinese script. Mervin's great-grandfather, Chong Sung, had built it during the previous century. For reasons of his own, his grandfather had given up his dreams of finding gold and of returning to China as a wealthy man. Instead, he had built the joss house in which to pursue the religion of his homeland. As per his wishes, and those of his descendants, the joss house had been preserved over the years by the family.

In the shadow of the joss house was the modest little home in which Mervin Hee had spent the early years of his life. After calling on his remaining family there, Mervin walked to the top of a nearby hill and visited the grave of his father in what he believed to be the most beautiful cemetery in the world. And there, beneath two wind-bent cypress trees, overlooking a breathtaking meeting of ocean and rocky shore, he lingered awhile, recalling his father's words.

"You must go to college, Mervin. Don't work in the mill, you need an education."

You were right, Father.

The South Delta was a tough, highly demanding district, but Mervin took to the job instantly, and for nine marathon years he cut a wide swath through the ranks of the violators there. He loved being a warden, reveled in it, but he still wasn't home. He longed for the sea and Mendocino County, and now and then he would summon the vision of himself driving his patrol truck across Two Log Creek.

In 1988, the Fort Bragg warden position in Mendocino County came open, and Mervin was among the first to apply for it. And he suffered again the crushing anxiety of wanting something desperately, but realizing that his chances were only fair at best. But some things are simply meant to be, and in early November, Mervin received word that the position was his.

And so it was that Mervin Hee, on a clear November morning, his first as the warden assigned to the Mendocino County coast, chose to visit the special place on the cliffs of the South Headlands of Caspar Bay.

I did it, Grandfather! I made it happen.

———————

At daybreak that November morning, shortly before Mervin Hee's arrival at Caspar Bay, a white van had appeared at a cliff top parking area across the bay from the South Headlands. The only vehicle present at that early hour, it paused only briefly, enough time to disgorge a single, large, wetsuit-clad individual wearing sneakers and a 20-pound weight belt.

Doyle Dean Malstrom was a poacher, a professional outlaw, an expert at converting wildlife into dollars. He peered warily around as he hurriedly dragged a duffle bag of gear and a single SCUBA tank through the side door of the van. He then slammed the door and called to the driver.

"You'll be back here at 9:30 sharp, right?"

The driver nodded and drove away. Malstrom shouldered the tank, snatched up the bag and headed for the edge of the cliff.

A narrow trail angled down the face of the cliff at this place, and as Malstrom started down, he spared hardly a glance at the sea surging around the jagged rocks a full 90 feet below. He proceeded cautiously, choosing his footing with care, for the trail was steep and hazardous. It ultimately descended to a narrow beach amid a tumble of boulders and exposed bedrock.

Upon reaching the beach, Malstrom hurried to a concealed spot amid the rocks and set about getting into the rest of his gear. After stashing the duffle bag in the rocks, and after swapping his sneakers for a pair of neoprene "booties," he strapped on the tank, grabbed his fins, a large mesh bag and an abalone iron and headed for the water. Moving carefully amid the slippery rocks and eelgrass, he chose a boulder in shallow water on which to sit briefly while he strapped on his fins. And as he rose and shuffled out into deeper water, the morning sun glinted off his SCUBA tank.

———————

It was the flash of sunlight on metal that brought Warden Mervin Hee out of his thoughts and focused his attention on the rocky shoreline on the north side of the bay. Raising his binoculars to his eyes, he was just in time to see a SCUBA diver entering the water. Immediately suspicious, he scanned the area for a second diver. There was none that he could see.

He hurried back to his patrol vehicle and drove out to the highway, and as he headed north around the bay, his mind raced. He was certain that a single SCUBA diver slipping into the water at first light in an area jammed with red abalone had to be up to no good. Not only was abalone season closed, but it was illegal to use SCUBA gear to harvest them.

As he neared the North Headlands of the bay, Mervin Hee reveled in the fact that he knew the area intimately, having grown up here. He knew where the diver would be parked. He knew the trail leading down to the rocky beach, and he even knew the sea bottom where the diver was doing whatever it was he was there to do.

Upon reaching the parking area near the cliffs, Mervin was not surprised to find it empty. He was glad of it, in fact, for it bolstered his certainty that he was onto a serious violator. *Why else would he be dropped off?*

Mervin hid his truck well away from the parking lot and set out on foot. At the cliff's edge, he scanned the scene below to determine that the diver was still submerged. He then started down the treacherous trail to the beach. Nothing had changed during his 12-year absence. He still knew every turn in the trail, each bad spot, and upon reaching the beach, he remembered the lay of the boulders there.

He had no trouble locating the diver's duffle bag stashed in the rocks. And after gleaning what information was available on the beach, he decided the best place to await the diver's return would be back on top of the cliffs. He therefore hurried back up the trail and took up a position on the damp grass at the cliff's edge. There was still no sign of the diver.

Using his binoculars, Mervin scanned the surface for the diver's bubble train, but he couldn't locate it. Then he noticed several gulls diving repeatedly at the same small area on the surface. Directing his binoculars on that place, he then spotted the bubbles. *But why the gulls?* Then it dawned on him.

———————

In the shadowy depths of Caspar Bay, Malstrom had found abalone immediately. It was just as Grider had said it would be. Grider, a commercial urchin diver, had encountered the place the day before while diving for urchins from his boat. He had encountered unusual numbers of abalone there and had informed Malstrom.

Malstrom knew well that a diver willing to take chances could clear a thousand dollars a day poaching abalone, so he decided to act immediately. He and Grider had devised their plan, and it was Grider, the following day, who dropped Malstrom off at the correct spot.

Malstrom now worked swiftly on the sea bottom near the kelp beds. Having already pried off more abalone than his mesh bag would hold, he was now "shucking" the abalone, prying them from their shells in order to save space in the bag for more of the valuable meat. And as he did so, torn bits of abalone meat and entrails drifted to the surface. He was unaware of the meal he was providing the sea birds 18 feet above.

Checking his air gage, Malstrom found he was out of time, so he stuffed all of the shucked abalone into the mesh bag and as many of the whole abalone as it would hold, and he started for shore. Upon reaching shallow water, he removed his fins, tilted his face mask back on his forehead and searched the beach and cliff top for any potential witnesses who might be about. Seeing none, he started for the beach, stumbling through the slippery shallows and dragging the heavy bag behind him.

At his hiding spot in the rocks, he shed all of his gear except for his wetsuit, enjoying the relief of being free of the heavy weight belt. He then put on his sneakers, shouldered the mesh bag of abalone and started for the path. As he labored up the trail, he mentally calculated the value of the 70 or so pounds of abalone in the bulging mesh bag.

Mervin Hee had seen it all and had verified by sight that the bag held illegally harvested abalone. He now prepared himself for the encounter which somehow he sensed would not go well. He had noted grimly that the outlaw was a large man, but fortunately Mervin Hee, at six feet and 225 pounds, was one of the larger wardens in the state.

Mervin chose an ambush site well back from the cliff. For he knew that the outlaw, if given the opportunity, would likely head for the cliff to throw the illegal evidence into the sea. With this possibility reasonably covered, all was ready. So Mervin waited for the outlaw to appear at the top of the trail. And while he had never in his adult life experienced fear of another human being, the pre-encounter butterflies he knew so well were now fluttering madly in the pit of his stomach.

First, the head of Doyle Dean Malstrom appeared at the top of the trail, then more of him, until all six-foot-two and 215 pounds of him was striding through the grass toward the hidden warden. The mesh bag bounced heavily on his back. Mervin waited until the man was a mere 10 feet away before he stood up.

"Good morning, sir! State Game Warden!"

Malstrom's response was instantaneous flight. Spinning around, he bolted for the cliff. Mervin sprinted after him, amazed at how effortlessly the man ran with the heavy bag. The chase ended a few feet from the edge of the cliff, when Mervin caught him from behind. Dragged to a stop, Malstrom struggled wildly. Mervin attempted to leg-sweep him, but could not maintain a hold on the damp, slippery wetsuit. But he had a firm grip on the mesh bag.

It now became a fierce tug-of-war for the mesh bag full of abalone, with Malstrom having the advantage of both the downward sloping terrain and of strength borne of desperation. Grunting and driving backwards with his powerful legs, Malstrom dragged Mervin closer and closer to the edge of the cliff. Suddenly they were on the brink, and Mervin knew with certainty that he was about to be dragged to his death. He then did the only thing he could do to save himself. He let go of the bag. Malstrom was launched backwards into space, still clinging to the bag, his eyes wide with terror. He plummeted end over end, landing head first in the water far below.

Horrified, Mervin peered down at Malstrom's motionless body as it surfaced. It floated face up, buoyed by the unweighted wetsuit, one hand still remarkably clutching the abalone bag. *Is he dead?* Then, to Mervin's vast relief, Malstrom began to move. Now his eyes were open, blinking tentatively, and they fixed immediately on the warden peering down at him from the cliff top.

"Are you okay?" Mervin shouted.

But Malstrom didn't answer. Instead, he rolled over onto his stomach and began swimming feebly out to sea. And as he did so, he loosened the drawstring on the bag and began dumping the abalone. Mervin could do nothing but watch. He called out several times to the man, ordering him ashore, but he was ignored. Mervin then hiked down to the beach and began gathering up Malstrom's diving gear. It was only then that Malstrom reluctantly swam ashore, shaken, but apparently unhurt.

"You're under arrest," said Mervin, as the man waddled toward him through the shallows.

"For what?" said Malstrom, holding up the empty mesh bag. "You don't have any evidence!"

"We'll see about that," said Mervin.

Two hours later, Mervin marched Malstrom, handcuffed and still wearing his wetsuit, into the booking cage at the Fort Bragg City Jail. Greeted by good-natured laughter, Mervin turned and was surprised and delighted to see that two of the jailers, young officers his age, were classmates from high school.

"I always *figured* you guys would end up in jail!" he said with a grin.

During the booking process, Mervin happened to overhear the police 911 dispatcher beginning emergency notifications for a missing diver. An urchin diver, one Raymond Grider, had reported the missing man. Putting two and two together, Mervin was able to quickly confirm from the dispatcher that not only was the missing diver very much alive, but that he was safely encaged a few yards away in their booking facility.

Upon leaving the jail, Mervin concerned himself with the urgent business of recovering the evidence lying on the bottom of Caspar Bay. He returned to the bay, equipped with wetsuit and snorkeling gear, and in short order he recovered 32 shucked abalone and a number of others still in the shell and alive, but upside down on the bottom.

All in all it was a great case, a fine homecoming for him in his new district. But one thing remained to be done.

The sun was low over the Pacific as the green patrol truck ground its way down the rutted road through the forested canyon, Warden Mervin Hee behind the wheel.

Little had changed in the quarter century or so of the warden's absence, except that a bridge now spanned the still-sparkling waters of Two Log Creek. As he neared the bridge, he hesitated a moment then cut the wheel to the left, steering the vehicle off the bridge approach and onto the abandoned bit of road that led to the shallow-water ford. Driving to the water's edge, he hesitated again, this time coming to a full stop.

He remained there for a while, lost in thought, the day's last rays of sunlight glinting off the shined, six-pointed silver star on his chest and illuminating the prowling golden bears on the blue and gold patches on his sleeves.

Then Warden Mervin Hee, third-generation American and great-grandson to one of the most tenacious and courageous immigrants this country has ever known, slipped the vehicle into low gear and drove forward.

The lugged wheels churned and water flew as the patrol truck plowed across.

I did it, Grandfather! I made it happen!

NOTHIN' PERSONAL

It was winter-comin'-cold in the mountains, and wisps of steam rose from the skinned and gutted carcass of an outlaw-killed deer.

There was no proof, as yet, that the deer had been illegally killed, but Warden Rennie Cleland, California Department of Fish and Game, would have bet his badge on it. He examined the animal closely where it hung, rope-tied by its antlers to a beam nailed between two fir trees. It was a good-size mule deer, a three-point buck, and whoever had killed it had made a good shot of it.

But something was definitely wrong. Cleland had sensed it immediately upon stepping from his patrol truck at the remote and hidden camp. Children were at play there, four bundled-up preschool kids, apparently carefree. But two bearded men, the only adults present, appeared anything but carefree upon finding a warden in their midst.

True, the deer appeared to be legally tagged, and a week of deer season yet remained in northern Siskiyou County. But even after recovering from their initial surprise, there was something in the demeanor of the two men that didn't ring true. Their attempts at acting "normal" and unconcerned were belied by a strong underlying tension.

"This is a nice buck," said Cleland. "Who's the lucky hunter?"

"My son, Troy, got it," said the larger of the two men, his voice a deep, guttural growl. "He got it this morning."

He stood easily six feet tall, big-boned, heavily muscled, a formidable-looking character. He reminded Cleland of Bluto from the Popeye cartoons. His companion, except for the beard, was an unremarkable average-guy type. Cleland put them both in their late thirties.

Looking closer at the deer, Cleland noted the expert way in which the meat had been cared for. *Lots of practice*, he thought. He untied the tag from the antlers and read the name. Troy Andrew Cosnoe. It struck a distant note in his memory, but he couldn't place it.

"I'd better validate this for him," said Cleland. "Where is he?"

"He's with his mother in town," said the man. "They went in to buy groceries." The man was hesitant to meet Cleland's gaze.

"When do you expect them back?" Cleland asked, now peering around and studying the camp. He noted the black and white pickup, beside which was a cab-over camper, standing on jacks.

"Could be any time," said the man. "My wife's hard to predict."

"How old is your son?"

"He's 14."

Cleland continued gently prodding the two men for information, and his certainty grew that they were up to no good. When he asked to see their hunting licenses and deer tags, presumptuous of him since they were not, at that time, hunting, the smaller of the two men produced a valid hunting license. But he had no deer tag. Instead, he showed Cleland a bear tag. The name on the license and tag read "John G. Burton," a resident of Oroville, some 200 miles to the south.

"You already got your deer this season?" Cleland asked.

"I got one on opening weekend," said Burton. But Cleland was certain that any nice buck that crossed Burton's path in the next few days, while the man was armed with rifle and bear tag, would not survive the experience.

Upon examining the larger man's license, the man's name brought him up short. Clayton J. Cosnoe. *Clayton Cosnoe*, he thought. Then it dawned on him. He knew the name because no fewer than three outraged hunters had warned him about this man whom they claimed bragged openly of killing several deer a year.

According to the license, Cosnoe, too, lived in Oroville. As Cleland searched his memory for all he had been told of the man, he examined Cosnoe's yet-unused deer tags and returned them to him.

"What town did your wife go to?" Cleland asked.

"Either Newell or Mount Hebron," said Cosnoe.

"I think they went to Mount Hebron," said Burton.

"I think they went to Oroville," piped one of the children, and Cosnoe cringed.

In view of who he was dealing with, Cleland now took some unusual steps. He began by taking a carcass temperature of the deer. Using his pocket knife, he made a narrow but deep incision into one hindquarter of the deer. He then inserted a thermometer into the cut. As he waited for the thermometer to rise and settle, he began filling out field identification cards on each man.

"What are you doing all *this* for?" said Cosnoe.

"Nothin' personal," said Cleland. "Just doin' my job."

As he finished the ID cards, Cleland asked each man for his home phone number. Burton readily provided his number, but Cosnoe hesitated. And when he came up with a number, Cleland got the definite feeling it would prove false.

Cleland turned to the deer again and checked the thermometer. He recorded the temperature on a note pad, then took the air temperature as well. Using this information and a carcass cooling chart, he would later determine the approximate time of death of the deer. According to the deer tag, the animal had been killed at 8:30 that morning. He was inclined to believe this, but in case the deer had been spotlighted during the night, he would soon know it.

"I'm gonna go ahead and validate this deer," said Cleland. "But I'll need to stop back here later and talk to your son."

Cosnoe nodded in understanding, but he was looking none too happy as Cleland climbed into his truck and drove away.

Upon leaving the camp, Cleland's intention was to get to a phone as fast as he could and call Cosnoe's home. It was critical to do so before Cosnoe beat him to it and warned his family. Cleland therefore headed straight for the little town of Tennant.

But Cleland had gone no farther than a mile when he encountered a situation he couldn't ignore. Upon rounding a bend, he came head-on to a pickup truck stopped in the roadway, a rifle barrel protruding from the driver's window. At that instant, the driver spotted the Fish and Game truck and jerked the rifle back inside, and as Cleland slid to a stop, door to door with him, the man was frantically jacking rounds through his lever-action .30-30 to unload it. But he was too late. Cleland had seen it all.

Cleland, like most wardens, almost always cited anyone he found with loaded guns in vehicles, for loaded guns in cars and pickups contrive with alarming frequency to discharge and kill people. And so it was that Cleland was delayed for a while, writing a citation on the hood of his truck to a violator who not only had his rifle loaded in his pickup, but fully intended to commit the additional offense of shooting a deer from the vehicle. And it was while Cleland was so engaged that the black and white pickup bearing Cosnoe and the children came careening around the bend, making a beeline for town. Cleland could only watch in frustration as it shot by.

When finished with the road-hunter, Cleland drove on into Tennant and tried the telephone number Cosnoe had given him. As expected, it proved bogus. He then tried directory assistance in Oroville and got lucky. He dialed the number, and a youthful female voice answered. He asked to speak with Troy.

"He's not here. He's up north deer hunting," came a well-rehearsed reply.

Cleland, in disgust, left the phone booth, resigning himself to a more lengthy investigation at best. There was a good chance the case was now beyond salvage, but at least he could return to the camp the following day and hopefully talk to Troy Cosnoe.

But the middle of deer season is a demanding time for mountain wardens, and other business kept him away. Cosnoe and company made it back to Oroville unchallenged. And so it was, the following Monday night, that Cleland phoned for assistance from the wardens in Butte County. Running his finger down the warden roster, he located the number he wanted, reached for the phone and dialed.

Lieutenant James Halber was just coming through the door when the phone rang. He snatched up the receiver and was surprised to find himself talking to Rennie Cleland, the warden stationed in Dorris, near the Oregon border. While Halber had never worked with Cleland, he had met him before and was well aware of Cleland's reputation. Among hard-working wardens, Cleland was regarded as one of the best. The two men exchanged small talk for a while, then Cleland got down to business.

"Do you know a guy named Clayton Cosnoe?" he asked.

"I sure do," said Halber. "He's a bad one." He then told Cleland of an encounter he had experienced with Cosnoe years earlier. Halber had been driving along on mountain patrol at the time, and upon rounding a bend he had seen Cosnoe ahead, standing on a bridge over a stream. And as luck would have it, Cosnoe had chosen that exact moment to toss a beer bottle from the bridge. The bottle rose in a lazy arc, tumbling end over end, then fell to shatter on the rocks below. Halber had seen it all.

But Cosnoe had been in no mood to be cited for littering on that day. He had been hostile, verbally abusive and totally uncooperative as Halber first attempted to fill out the citation. It wasn't until Halber had obviously had enough of the man and had closed his citation book, preparing for war, that Cosnoe backed off to the point that Halber could resume writing, get the job done and depart.

"And we had another run-in with him not long ago," continued Halber. "He does some commercial fishing, and two of the wardens in my squad had to ask him some questions about his activities. He gave 'em a real hard time."

"I don't doubt it," said Cleland.

Cleland then told Halber the story of Cosnoe's suspicious activity in Siskiyou County and the buck tagged with Troy Cosnoe's tags.

"I was wondering if you could find out what school Troy Cosnoe goes to and determine whether or not he was there last Thursday."

"No problem," said Halber. "I'll do it first thing tomorrow."

True to his word, Halber was on the phone the following morning, and his task proved quite simple. He called the junior high school nearest to the Cosnoe address and asked to speak with the principal. Upon hearing Halber's explanation of the situation, the principal verified that Troy Cosnoe was indeed a student there, and that it would be no problem to check with the boy's teachers.

An hour later, the principal phoned back and informed Halber that all six of Troy Cosnoe's teachers had verified that the boy had been in classes all day on the preceding Thursday, the day the deer had been killed.

"But *here's* something interesting," said the principal. "Troy was absent all day on Friday, the *following* day. His mother called and told us that Troy had to attend his great-grandfather's funeral."

"That *is* interesting," said Halber. "But I'm not surprised. I'll bet his mother loaded him into the car and headed straight for Siskiyou County the minute his dad called them on Thursday afternoon."

Halber thanked the school principal for his help, then turned his mind to the question of what to do next. Clayton Cosnoe was as good as convicted. The deer had been fraudulently tagged, and Clayton Cosnoe had been in possession of it. It wasn't even necessary to prove who actually shot the deer.

But what if we could prove it? Halber thought. Halber could now remember having received information himself on Cosnoe, almost a year earlier, a complaint that Cosnoe had killed a deer and tagged it with his wife's tag. The caller had further stated that Cosnoe had committed the same violation each deer season for years. There was therefore an excellent chance, Halber knew, that the three-point buck tagged with Troy's tags was Cosnoe's *second* deer that year, that he could well have killed a deer during the first days of the season and tagged it with his wife's tag.

Halber also knew, from years of experience, that there was an excellent chance that the antlers from any deer Cosnoe had recently killed would be visible somewhere in his yard, on the roof of an outbuilding or hanging over a fence or a tree limb. He therefore planned a little scouting expedition.

An hour later, driving his private, unmarked pickup truck, Halber coasted by the Cosnoe residence in the rural, foothill country east of Oroville. The home was a well landscaped, expensive place with a large garage and several outbuildings including a sizeable barn with adjoining horse corrals. And there were expensive toys as well, a new jet-boat and trailer outfit, a motor home, and a new pickup. Halber saw no deer antlers, but then he hadn't expected antlers to be visible from the road.

Leaving Cosnoe's residence, Halber consulted a map and drove to a point about a half mile east of the house. Parking his truck there, he pulled on a camouflage shirt and hat, grabbed his binoculars and slipped into the oak and Digger pine forest. A few minutes of dodging trees and poison-oak put him on a hillside with a clear view of the rear of Cosnoe's lair. Peering through his binoculars, Halber studied the place for a few seconds, then smiled to himself. For there, on the back fence, hung three sets of fresh deer antlers, one of which, contrary to State law, bore no deer tags.

Returning to his own home, Halber phoned Rennie Cleland with the news. "Looks like Mr. Cosnoe is in a pickle," said Halber. "Troy was in school all day."

Cleland was pleased. Halber then told him of his scouting foray to Cosnoe's house and of the untagged deer antlers on the fence.

"I think we've got enough for a search warrant," said Halber. "This guy is a serious violator, and I think we should go after him."

"I agree," said Cleland.

The following day, Halber spent several intense hours at his word processor, hammering out the necessary elements of a search warrant. Then came a visit to the district attorney's office for *his* input and approval, then a search for a judge to sign it. It was mid-afternoon when Halber emerged from the superior court building, the signed document in hand.

Shortly before dark that same day, four Fish and Game patrol vehicles wheeled into Clayton Cosnoe's driveway. Doors flew open and six uniformed wardens jumped out and scattered to assigned locations around the house and outbuildings. Lieutenant Halber, bearing the warrant, climbed the front steps and knocked on the door. The door swung open, and there stood Clayton Cosnoe.

"Mr. Cosnoe? State Fish and Game. We have a warrant to search your residence," said Halber. He had expected anger and opposition from Cosnoe, but instead he saw only fear.

"What's this about?" said Cosnoe.

"It's about the deer you killed last Thursday and tagged with your son's tag."

There was a brief hesitation, then Cosnoe said, "Okay, I admit it. I killed the deer and put Troy's tag on it."

Halber was puzzled. Not only was he surprised over Cosnoe's instant confession, but he was puzzled over the man's present emotional state. He appeared to be terrified. And behind him, his wife, Jan, a tall, painfully slender, dark-haired woman appeared *equally* terrified.

"We're gonna have to come in, sir," said Halber.

Cosnoe and his wife stepped aside, and Halber, followed by three other wardens, walked into the front room. Halber assigned the wardens rooms to search.

"Can't you just issue me a citation? I admit I did it, and I'll take you to the meat," said Cosnoe.

"No sir, we still have to search," said Halber. "Would you and your wife please sit over here until we're finished?"

They did as they were told, and took seats at a kitchen table. Looking at the two, Halber was thoroughly amused. Rennie Cleland had told him that Clayton Cosnoe looked like Bluto from the Popeye cartoons, and now here sat the man's wife, string-bean skinny, her hair drawn back in a bun, looking just like Olive Oyl.

"What rifle did you use to kill the deer?" asked Halber, suppressing any sign of mirth.

"I used my .30-06," said Cosnoe. "It's over there."

Halber retrieved an old and battered rifle with an equally battered scope. But in a glass-fronted gun cabinet, several rifles and shotguns were visible, one of them a beautiful, scoped, Browning .270 semi-automatic.

As the investigation continued, one of the wardens brought the three sets of deer antlers to the front door. One set bore no tags at all. One set, a three-point, was tagged with Troy's tags. And the third set, a nice four-point with an oddly twisted eye guard, was tagged with Cosnoe's tags.

"So, you killed another deer after the one you tagged with Troy's tags?" Halber asked.

"Yeah, I'll admit that too," said Cosnoe. "I shot it the next day."

"What about the set of antlers with no tag?" Halber asked.

"My wife killed that one on opening day," said Cosnoe. "She tagged it. The tags are around here someplace."

Jan Cosnoe did find the tags, and despite considerable questioning by Halber, she clung to the story that she had killed the deer. Halber didn't believe it, but there was no way to prove otherwise. However, the deer tag had not been validated, and it had been illegally detached from the antlers. So Jan Cosnoe would indeed pay a price as well for her share in the deception.

At this point, Warden Leonard Blissenbach called to Halber from the master bedroom. Halber hurried there and found the warden weighing a plastic sandwich bag full of dried, leafy plant material on an Ohaus triple-beam scale.

"Exactly one ounce," said Blissenbach. "Obviously for sale. I found the marijuana and the scale together in a chest of drawers in the closet."

Cosnoe and his wife now looked nauseous as well as terrified. And the arrival of Reserve Wardens Lee and Teagarden reporting a locked room in the barn—a room in which they could hear some kind of machinery running—did nothing to improve their spirits.

"We'll need a key for that room," said Halber.

Cosnoe, looking desperate, first claimed that he had lost the key to the room. But he thought better of it when Halber explained that without a key, the wardens would be forced to use a crowbar. Cosnoe reluctantly provided the key.

Back in the barn, Warden Lee applied the key to the lock, swung open the door and gazed in upon a 12 by 12-foot room with white-painted sheet-rocked walls. A huge light bulb and reflector hung from the ceiling, its powerful glare illuminating 27 adult marijuana plants below. There was a large ventilating fan, a ballast unit to run the light, a drip irrigation system and timers. It was a classic "grow room," right out of the book entitled *Indoor Marijuana Horticulture* that Warden Blissenbach was soon to find in the master bedroom.

Within a few minutes of the discovery of the grow room, Clayton Cosnoe found himself in handcuffs, seatbelted in Blissenbach's patrol vehicle and on his way to Butte County Jail. Upon his arrival, when the heavy steel door of the booking cage clattered shut behind him, he was finally struck by the full, shocking realization of what his greed had brought down upon himself and his family.

When finished with their search, the wardens provided Jan Cosnoe with a receipt for the evidence seized. This evidence included the marijuana, the equipment from the grow room, a variety of photos and undeveloped film, and a number of rifles and shotguns. There were 11 long guns in all, all seized because the simple deer case had now become a felony drug case. Of the 11 guns found in the home, three turned out to be stolen. The three deer carcasses were found, as Cosnoe had said they would be, hanging at a nearby market. These, too, were seized.

Jan Cosnoe watched as the procession of patrol vehicles drove away, turning north from her driveway, headed for town. And it was then her tears began to fall.

To the Siskiyou County district attorney, Warden Rennie Cleland provided a report on the Cosnoe case that was like *all* of his reports—bullet-proof. And Cosnoe's defense attorney could see no effective way to defend his client.

Cosnoe had stuck with his claim that he had shot both illegal deer with the old .30-06, in hopes of saving his new and much beloved Browning. But Cleland had thwarted this effort by producing a series of three photos from exposed film seized from a camera during the search.

The first photo in the series showed Cosnoe sneaking along a dirt road, rifle at the ready, apparently stalking a deer. The second photo showed him aiming the rifle at something in the forest. The third photo showed him, rifle in hand, kneeling beside a downed four-point buck with an oddly twisted eye guard. And in each photo, the rifle was not the battered .30-06, but clearly the new .270 Browning.

In the end, a plea bargain settled the matter. In exchange for dropping charges against Jan Cosnoe and Cosnoe's friend, Burton, whom Cleland had charged with obstructing an officer, Cosnoe pled guilty. The resulting sentence cost him well over $2,000, not counting a similar amount in attorney fees. And he would still answer to felony drug charges in Butte County.

As he shuffled from the courtroom, a beaten man, he encountered Cleland on the street.

"I guess you got me *good*," he said.

Rennie Cleland, always the professional, regarded the man briefly and replied, "Strictly business, Mr. Cosnoe. Nothin' personal."

Bottom Feeders

A bloody gravel bar. Scattered shell casings. To Warden Rick Banko, Department of Fish and Game, it appeared as though a battle had been fought here. The evidence of violent conflict lay everywhere, in stark contrast to the quiet beauty of the surroundings. The Klamath River, deep and silent at this spot, glided by in its bed of gray granite. A dense forest of moss-barked fir and tall redwoods flanked the river and swept skyward up steep canyon walls.

The scene of what appeared to be a wildlife crime was much as George Salter had described. Salter, an agent with the Bureau of Indian Affairs (BIA), had happened onto the spot and returned to town and phoned Banko.

"It looks like some poacher killed a deer or a bear there," he said.

Banko, wasting no time, had hopped into the big inboard-powered jet boat and headed upriver. The sun was high overhead on this clear summer day. The cool river air had a taste all its own, which Banko drank in with pure pleasure. Tall, dark-haired, clean-cut, Banko could have been a Marine on a recruiting poster. And at age 31, only three years into the career he loved and had fought so hard to attain, he had already earned the reputation for being one of the best of his trade.

Blasting up the riffles and skimming over the drifts, he made short work of the eight-mile run to the gravel bar described by Salter. The bar lay on the edge of a deep depression in the river bottom known along the coast as County-Line Hole. Upon examining the gravel bar, Banko knew instantly that it had not been a deer that had been killed there. Nor had it been a bear. A few seconds of hard scrutiny revealed that some of the blood smears were much fresher than others. It was obvious that more than one animal had been killed, and on different days.

Banko's attention was then drawn to several grooves or furrows in the sand at the edge of the bar. It appeared that several heavy objects had been dragged from the water here and up onto the gravel bar. Then something else caught his eye, a tangle of heavy monofilament fishing line. Examining it, he concluded that it had to be at least 100 lb. test line. A few feet away, more heavy line lay amid the cobbles, and this time there were hooks attached—three large treble hooks. But these hooks had been mangled, several of the points straightened. Then it dawned on him. *Sturgeon!* It had to be sturgeon.

It all made sense now. Nick Albert, the warden in Arcata, had found sturgeon heads and entrails dumped at Little River, along Highway 101. They had been green sturgeon, the rarer of the two species found in California. In fact, the only place within 50 miles where green sturgeon could be found was the Klamath River. They had to be Klamath River fish, probably cleaned at Little River. Banko could picture now how their deaths had come about—the big fish snagged with treble hooks, dragged near the bank, shot with guns, then dragged ashore, their heavy bodies plowing furrows in the sand. As he counted the furrows—seven, eight, nine—his anger grew.

But anger would be of no help in bringing down the sturgeon killers. It would take patience and cunning. Fortunately, Banko had plenty of each. His anger was soon replaced by a cold unshakable resolve. He would catch these outlaws. He would make them pay, whether it took a day or a year.

The river here made a hard, nearly right-angle turn to the left. Spilling down Upper Lamm's Riffle, the water struck a high wall of granite and was deflected left into the 50-foot depths of County-Line Hole. The killing place, the gravel bar on which Banko stood, was on the inside of the turn. A few yards from the river the land rose sharply, 10 feet or so. Banko hiked to the top of this rise and found himself on another, much wider gravel bar, the high-water flood plain of the river. From here he studied the surrounding terrain, planning how to use it to his advantage. But the terrain here would offer few advantages to the wardens.

Banko soon concluded that there was no good place near the hole from which to watch, so he turned his attention to the higher ground, farther back from the river. He stood there awhile, studying the blackberry and alder thickets, planning, calculating. The river whispered its quiet song. A raven croaked in the distance.

With his plan made, the details firmly in his mind, Banko returned to the jet boat. The big engine fired instantly, and with a burst of power in reverse, Banko backed off the bar into deep water. Swinging the bow down river, he shifted to forward thrust, leaned on the throttle, and with a roar the 21 feet of welded aluminum leaped ahead. In four seconds the boat was up on plane, and Banko sent it careening down Lower Lamm's Riffle toward home.

Banko had been gone only a short while when a battered, rust-ravaged pickup arrived. It rattled across the bar and stopped near the water. The doors swung open, and two of the nastiest-looking men on the planet stepped out and looked around. Incredibly filthy, heavily bearded, foul-smelling characters in bib overalls, they were typical of a lawless breed of dope-growing, game-poaching hillbillies that inhabited the more remote areas of the county. From the back of the pickup, they grabbed heavy fishing outfits and stalked to the water's edge. Each fishing rod was equipped with snag gear—large treble hooks above heavy weights. The men began casting far out into the deep hole and violently jerking the hooks back across the bottom.

Almost immediately, one set of hooks bit deeply into flesh.

––––––––

The fish was large for her breed, over seven feet from the tip of her shark-like tail to her shovel-shaped, whiskered snout. She had a grotesque, toothless mouth, underslung, classic of a bottom-feeder. But while short on beauty, her kind had stood the test of time, and ancestors looking much like her had shared the world with dinosaurs. Like all green sturgeon, she was a sea-going creature, more so than her cousins, the white sturgeon, that preferred bays and estuaries. She herself had scavenged the soft-bottomed areas off the Pacific Coast for nearly half a century, and she had returned eight times during her life to spawn in the river where her life had begun. If she survived, she would spawn again. But for now, her survival was very much in doubt.

At the first bite of steel hooks into her body, she rushed to the surface and leaped like a marlin. Striking the water with an enormous splash, she dove to the deepest part of the pool. And there she fought for her life. She was strong, and she weighed nearly 200 pounds, but the steady pressure drawing her shoreward was relentless. Forty-five minutes into the fight she was noticeably tiring and was drawn dangerously near shore. But she fought her way back to deep water, thrashing and twisting. Then again she was drawn shoreward. The man clutching the rod and reel tightened his drag, sensing victory. His companion grabbed a Magnum pistol, took aim at her head and fired.

But it was a bad shot, the bullet only grazing her; however, the shock of the near miss stunned her. But only momentarily. With one final burst of energy, she again lunged for deep water, nearly dragging the snagger with her. And with this, the hooks in her back straightened and pulled free. The fishing weight, like a small cannon ball, shot back, narrowly missing the man with the rod. He ducked and fell backwards onto the gravel, cursing.

The fish retired to the darkest depths of the pool, her strength slowly returning. She bore a painful wound on her back and a bullet crease near her head, but she was alive. Others, however, would not fare so well.

———————

Late afternoon found Banko back at his home in Klamath. He sat at his desk, a telephone to his ear, in conversation with his supervisor. Lieutenant Steve Conger listened with great interest as Banko explained the situation.

"I think we should stake it out," said Banko.

"I agree," said Conger, and within the hour he had arranged for help to send with Banko. Ordinarily he would have insisted on going himself, which would have pleased Banko, but he was tied up on other business. Instead, he arranged for Larry Bruckenstein to go. Bruckenstein was the Garberville warden, far to the south, but he was on temporary assignment to Crescent City on Field Training Officer duty. He was providing training for new warden Paul Weldon, who had just been assigned there. Conger felt that Bruckenstein and Weldon would be plenty of help for Banko, and it would be a great opportunity for Weldon to hang out for a while with two highly respected wardens and to learn about stakeouts.

The following afternoon, the three wardens met and took Highway 101 south out of Klamath. An hour before dark, along the highway, Banko unlocked a big iron gate guarding an entrance to Simpson Timber Company land. They then headed inland on a confusing system of dirt roads. A dozen twisted miles later, with the two patrol vehicles hidden near Upper Lamm's Riffle, the three wardens headed on foot to a spot Banko had chosen the day before. By dark, they were settled down to wait in a nest they had hollowed in a blackberry patch overlooking the gravel bar above County-Line Hole.

As the hours passed, Banko and Bruckenstein, as wardens invariably do, began telling "war stories." Warden Trainee Paul Weldon listened with rapt attention as the two men exchanged tale after tale of wardens tangling with various outlaws on the North Coast. One such story, a favorite among local wardens, involved Steve Conger, who at the time was the warden newly assigned to Orleans. It involved Conger's arrest of Nathan Ludwig, the elder of the infamous Ludwig clan. Conger had left his patrol vehicle and hiked down into a canyon to arrest Ludwig for sturgeon snagging on the Klamath River. Ludwig, who was accustomed to intimidating others and who had the well-deserved reputation for being highly dangerous, had fixed Conger with cold gray eyes and said, "You know, Mr. Warden, only one of us'll be walkin' outta here today."

Conger had returned a stare every bit as chilly and said, "Since I'm wearin' the gun, I guess that'll be me." This story, first circulated among the Ludwig clan, then reached the other wardens, and finally it was reluctantly confirmed by Conger.

The war stories continued until well past midnight when a light rain began to fall. The wardens then began shifts, one keeping watch while the others curled up in their camo rain gear and catnapped. But dawn, cold and wet, found the situation unchanged, the sturgeon of County-Line Hole unmolested.

The second night of the stakeout was a repeat of the first. More cold, more damp, more war stories, but no action. On the chance that the outlaws could be brash enough to do their dirty work during daylight, the wardens agreed to stay with the stakeout for a while longer. But by mid-afternoon, Bruckenstein had to admit that he could no longer justify keeping Weldon away from his training. He and Weldon then said their goodbyes to Banko and headed back for Crescent City. But Banko remained, having chosen to stick with the stakeout at least until dark.

Dissatisfied with the poor visibility from the blackberry patch, Banko decided to move. Hiking back to his patrol truck, he drove to a higher road where he hid the vehicle again, this time near a log landing that afforded a distant but direct view of County-Line Hole and the bloody gravel bar. He had been there no more than an hour when the situation suddenly changed.

He had been sitting in his patrol truck, a clipboard on his lap, laboring over some paperwork he had brought along, when the sound of an approaching vehicle brought him up short. He heard it pass on a nearby road and continue toward the river. Then it appeared on the upper gravel bar, a battered blue pickup truck jammed with people. Grabbing his binoculars, he watched as it rattled along, approaching the water. The driver negotiated the descent to the lower bar, where he stopped. Banko counted two women and several children as they climbed out of the pickup bed, and two men stepped from the cab.

Having parked so that his patrol truck was all but invisible from the river, Banko was able to use his window-mounted spotting scope. Clamping it to his partially raised window, he squinted through it and focused on the pickup. He was in time to see both men grab heavy ocean-fishing outfits from the vehicle and head for the water.

They walked to a sand spit opposite the deepest part of the hole, and as they readied their gear, Banko could clearly see that they were outlaws. They were using giant treble hooks and round lead weights the size of golf balls. They used no bait or lures, obviously intending to snag fish. After casting as far across the deep pool as they could, they retrieved the heavy rigs by means of violent, sweeping jerks with their rods, reeling in between jerks.

Banko reached for his radio mike and called Bruckenstein and Weldon. Fortunately he caught the two men just as they were arriving in Crescent City.

"They're here," said Banko. "Two of 'em . . . and a couple of women."

Weldon immediately wheeled the patrol vehicle around and again headed south. Most would have preferred a hot meal first after being out all night, but Bruckenstein never gave it a thought. And Weldon, with the limitless zeal of a rookie, couldn't have been happier. Warden Don Kelly, who had been checking boats in Crescent City Harbor, also heard the radio traffic, and he too headed south. But they had a long way to go.

Banko now stowed the spotting scope and drove to a hidden spot near Lamm's Riffle. He then set out on foot to get closer to the snaggers. Soon he had them in sight again, and he now watched them through his binoculars. Nothing had changed. They were still doing their best to snag a sturgeon. After a half hour or so, Banko decided to get yet closer, a move that would require several minutes' time. Keeping to the brush, careful to stay out of sight, he circled part of the bar and began searching for a better vantage point. But then a pistol shot rang out, and he sprinted to a place where he could again see the suspects.

One of the suspects stood braced on the gravel bar, his fishing rod bent in a tight arc. The second suspect, pistol in hand, appeared to be waiting for another shot at what was undoubtedly a sturgeon on his companion's line. Ten minutes passed as the struggle between man and fish continued. The man was gaining on the fish, slowly pumping the rod, then dropping the tip and taking a few turns on the reel. Then suddenly the fish surfaced a few feet from shore, thrashing its tail and rolling. The man reared back on the rod, and the fish lost ground, tail first. Then the man with the pistol waded in, took aim and fired. Water erupted in a tall geyser, and the big fish went limp. They then dragged the fish ashore, across the gravel, and hid it among some low bushes.

Banko was prepared to go in alone, if necessary, if the snaggers attempted to leave. But the snaggers, upon dealing with the first fish, took up their fishing gear, walked down to the water and went at it again. A short time later, Banko's hand-held radio came alive.

"We're here," said Warden Bruckenstein. "Where do you want us?"

Due to the lay of the land, the suspects would be out of sight for a few minutes when the wardens made their approach. Banko therefore suggested that one of the wardens remain where he could keep the suspects in view. This duty went to Kelly. Bruckenstein and Weldon hiked down and met with Banko. By chance, the timing on all of this was perfect, for no sooner had the other wardens arrived than the snaggers called it quits. One of them went to the pickup and backed it toward the sturgeon they had killed earlier.

"Let's do it," said Banko, and the three wardens set off at a trot. Down the road to the bar they went, and upon breaking into the open, they slowed and spread out. Acting on Banko's signals, they crept to the edge of the upper bar and arrived in time to see the two suspects loading the sturgeon into the back of the pickup. Engrossed in this chore, the suspects never saw the wardens slipping up on them. The wardens were a mere 15 feet away when Banko, half crouched, his hand on his pistol butt, caught their attention.

"STATE GAME WARDENS! GET YOUR HANDS UP!"

The suspects leaped and spun around, dropping the sturgeon. Had they been zapped with cattle prods their reactions could not have been more spectacular. They stood gasping for breath.

"GET YOUR HANDS UP!" Banko repeated, and *this* time they complied. "WHERE'S THE GUN?" Bruckenstein found the gun in the front seat of the pickup, and only then did Banko allow the suspects to relax.

Elroy Ludwig, the larger of the two outlaws and the son of the infamous Nathan Ludwig, was first to recover from his fright.

"We didn't do nothin' wrong," he said, in the first of a dozen or so less-than-credible statements proclaiming his innocence. Others included, "Someone else caught that fish," "We just got here," and "I'm an Indian," this last in reference to the fact that County-Line Hole was on an Indian reservation. But a BIA agent who arrived shortly thereafter was quick to point out that Elroy Ludwig was no Indian. The second outlaw, John Kramm, remained grimly silent.

The women and children had returned to the pickup just as the wardens began writing citations. And while the men stood sullenly, taking their medicine, the women began chipping away at the wardens.

"Don't you have nothin' better to do than scarin' babies?" "Why don't ya just shoot us!" And the chipping then degraded to simple name calling—names of the most vile sort. The wardens bore this abuse in silence, finished their paperwork, collected their evidence and departed.

Two days later, Banko drove seven hours to Fish and Game's Wildlife Investigations Laboratory near Sacramento. Packed in ice in the rear of his vehicle was the five-foot sturgeon killed by

Ludwig and Kramm. James D. Banks, Staff Wildlife Pathologist, a man of vast knowledge and experience, awaited him there to examine the sturgeon. Soon Banks, in his long white lab coat, had the sturgeon under close scrutiny on a stainless steel necropsy table. After a brief search, Banks was able to do what the wardens had failed to do— locate the hook wounds among the bony plates along the fish's back. Prodding gently with a dissecting needle, he manipulated the plates until two deep punctures were visible. He then compared one of the large treble hooks to the wounds and found that the distance between the hook points exactly matched the distance between the hook wounds on the sturgeon.

"It's a perfect match," he said. "Two points of one of the hooks got him."

Banks then carefully examined the tissue in and around the fish's mouth and found no wounds or tears of any kind. Nor were there any line marks near the head. Behind the dorsal fin, near the hook wounds, there were several long, straight lines that were in fact bruises in the fish's skin caused by fishing line under heavy tension.

"This is great evidence," said Banks. "This fish was snagged."

Upon returning to Klamath, Banko arranged for Bruckenstein and Joaquin Mariante, certified Fish and Game divers, to dive County-Line Hole and look for more evidence. There was a good chance that the divers could recover a bullet fired at the sturgeon— a bullet that could be linked to the big revolver the wardens had seized from Ludwig's pickup. But they were disappointed in their search for bullets. They did, however, explore the hole, and they were amazed to find the bottom littered with hundreds of weights and snag hooks of all description, the accumulation of years of illegal snagging.

At one point, as Bruckenstein descended to the deepest part of the hole, he disturbed something very large which shot away in a cloud of silt. At the same time, Banko, who had been looking on from the gravel bar, was astounded to see a seven-foot sturgeon erupt from the depths and beach itself in the shallow water in front of him. Thrashing and rolling, it soon reached deep water again, but not before Banko noticed what looked like a bullet crease near the fish's head.

The jury trial of Elroy Ludwig and John Kramm was a two-day affair. The defense, financed by a dope-growing member of the Ludwig clan, was the best the North Coast had to offer. Thornton J. Coswell, a veteran defense attorney, was totally ruthless at his work, and he boasted an impressive list of freed criminals to his credit. His specialty was confusing juries and vilifying cops. He hated cops and anyone else who wore a badge.

Pitted against this legendary bully of the local legal world was a petite young woman, mere weeks out of law school. Deputy District Attorney Ellen Chance, inexperienced and soft-voiced, had but two things going for her. First, she was brilliant, and second, she could meet Thornton Coswell's intimidating gaze with never a flinch.

In looking back on the trial, Banko would recall a number of things with great clarity. Not the least of these concerned Coswell's attempts to paint the arresting wardens as heavy-handed, gun-toting thugs. On cross-examining Warden Bruckenstein, Coswell had asked him how many rounds his duty pistol could contain. When the puzzled Bruckenstein answered "14," Coswell turned to the jury and said, "Enough bullets to kill everyone on that gravel bar!"

The wives of the defendants had testified as well, or rather they had perched in the witness chair and spat venom at the wardens, a performance that offended the jury. And of course there was the "phantom fisherman." Coswell had found another of the Ludwig clan to testify that he, not Elroy, had caught the sturgeon.

But the part of the trial that Banko would always marvel over was the testimony of Jim Banks, the wildlife pathologist from Sacramento. As Banks took the stand, the jury saw an unremarkable-looking fellow in his mid-forties. But when Ellen

Chance asked him his qualifications, the jury soon learned that his was a list of impressive qualifications that read like War and Peace. It went on . . . and on . . . and on.

And when he began his testimony concerning the sturgeon, it was immediately apparent that there was something in the man's voice and delivery that commanded attention and respect, something that exuded wisdom and truth, some difficult-to-define quality that brought many of the jurors forward in their seats, hanging on his every word. Perhaps it was his mastery of the subject or his awesome vocabulary or the fact that he was so very articulate. But whatever it was, it wove its spell on the jury and before long they would have blindly believed anything he said.

On cross-examination, Coswell did his absolute best to confuse Banks, to trip him up, to shake his composure. But Banks was a rock. And he had a remarkable way of responding to Coswell's questions, a raised eyebrow perhaps or some subtle change in inflection, that could make the questions, and therefore Coswell, look foolish.

Coswell grew angry, and the madder he got, the more Banks quietly destroyed him. When Coswell finally gave it up, and Banks was excused by the judge, the courtroom nearly broke into applause. Banks smiled and nodded to the jury, then walked from the courtroom. Behind him, Coswell's carefully planned defense lay in utter ruin.

After only a short deliberation, the jury found the defendants guilty on all counts.

The big fish traveled another 20 miles upriver, and when she sensed the time was right, she moved into a fast-flowing riffle. And there, attended by several frenzied males, she emitted a stream of tiny eggs from her body. Thousands of eggs. Then hundreds of thousands of eggs. Finally over a million eggs, she spewed into the sperm-laden water. Within minutes they exuded a sticky film which bonded them instantly to any hard surface they encountered, and soon the river bottom was covered with tiny eggs.

But immediately other scavengers in the river began to feed on them, and the odds of an egg actually producing a young sturgeon were long indeed. But some would survive. In a year, the surviving hatchlings would be foot-long sturgeon in the lower river, armored with rows of razor-edged, bony plates, almost immune to predation. A year after that they would be two-footers and would leave the river and land behind to become sea creatures like their mother.

On a moonlit August night, following a near-fatal encounter with a gillnet, the big fish once again glided across the river bar to lose herself in the vast Pacific. Although wounded and scarred, she had defied great odds and survived. With luck she would return again.

An Outing with Team Taylor

"It ain't hard to outsmart Fish and Game," said Leland Krieberg. "You just gotta use your head."

Krieberg, his great girth wedged into a booth at a Redding pancake house, a smug look on his broad face, addressed a younger man across the table. Everything about Krieberg was big, including his voice, which carried clearly to the neighboring booth. Fish and Game Warden Gayland Taylor, off-duty in the neighboring booth, was deep in conversation with his two sons and missed Krieberg's comments. His wife, Nancy, however, did not. She nudged her husband, discreetly pointed in the direction of Krieberg, and mouthed the word, "Listen."

"Does it work the same with deer tags, or just antelope?" asked the younger man.

"It'll work for any of 'em," said Krieberg. "It's a snap with a name like mine. I just change a letter here, add a letter there, anything to screw up the computer. I sent in eight applications this year."

"Have you ever got an antelope before?"

"This'll be my third," said Krieberg. "Last year I got one on my daughter's tag. I'm goin' for a big one this year."

Taylor was a warden in Butte County, a long way from antelope country, but he knew that California's limited pronghorn antelope season opened the next day. And even Taylor's sons knew that you could submit only one application a year per hunter for the antelope drawings. Brooks, age 11, and Brian, 9, now listened with

83

amusement as the man in the next booth thoroughly incriminated himself.

Taylor found himself in the familiar quandary of how to separate business from pleasure. He and his family were on vacation, on their way to spend a few days on the Klamath River. But chance had again brought a situation to light that Taylor could not easily ignore. It happened often, and many a Taylor family outing had been strained by some violator inadvertently throwing himself at Taylor's feet. But Nancy was good about it, and the boys often found it something of an adventure watching their father deal with some luckless outlaw.

When a waitress arrived, miraculously balancing four complete breakfasts without benefit of tray or cart, she found the Taylors in quiet discussion. Taylor looked to his wife. Without hesitation, Nancy whispered, "This guy needs to be caught." A glance at the boys told Taylor that they were of like mind.

Assessing what he knew, Taylor concluded that there was no time to call for help. The suspect and his companion were nearly finished eating and would soon be gone. Taylor knew also that to make this case, the suspect would have to be caught while hunting with a fraudulently acquired antelope tag in his possession. This would require knowledge of where the suspect intended to hunt. Taylor knew then that there was no choice but to follow the man.

"Eat fast," said Taylor, as the waitress placed a bill on Krieberg's table. Almost immediately, Krieberg and his companion rose and headed for the cash register. As Taylor kept a nervous eye on the man, he and his family frantically attacked their breakfasts. And in mere seconds, as the waitress looked on in astonishment, the boys wolfed down their pancakes and eggs, and their parents demolished a pair of Belgian waffles. Taylor then leaped up, threw money on the table, and the family bolted for the door.

Congestion at the cash register and a restroom stop delayed Krieberg enough that the Taylors were able to reach the parking lot in time to see him and his friend depart in a white van. The Taylors piled into their pickup and camper shell and set out in pursuit, up the northbound on-ramp to Interstate 5. Once on the freeway, Taylor approached to within reading distance of the van's license plate. Nancy wrote as the boys called out the characters. Taylor then drifted back, taking up a position nearly a quarter mile behind the van.

Ordinarily the Taylor boys would grow a bit cranky on a long trip. But on this day there was no bickering, for they shared a common purpose.

"Where do you think they're goin', Dad?" said Brooks.

"Probably somewhere around Tule Lake," said Taylor. Nancy then spread open a map, and while the boys looked on, wedged in the open boot between the cab and the camper shell, she traced the most likely route.

"They'll probably turn off on Highway 97 at Weed," she said. And she was right. Shortly after passing Mt. Shasta, its lofty top obscured in clouds of its own making, the van took the main off-ramp at the town of Weed.

"I hope they stop," said Brian. "I could use a pit stop." But the van continued straight through town and out toward the high-desert country beyond. Tailing the van now became more tricky, the chances of being "made" having greatly increased. Taylor therefore dropped farther back. But they were now approaching antelope country, and the chance of the van taking a side road off the highway increased with each passing mile.

Sure enough, as they descended into the Butte Valley, about 12 miles south of Dorris, Krieberg finally left the highway. Taylor was ready for it and spotted his brake lights immediately. Then dust billowed up as the van accelerated down an unpaved road. Taylor slowed, waited a solid minute, then set out after it.

Worried that the van could travel for miles on back roads before reaching its destination, Taylor was therefore delighted to top a rise and see that it had pulled into a camping area less than two miles from the highway. Taylor stopped and reached for the binoculars he always kept at hand. Through the binoculars, he had a good view of the van, and he watched for a few minutes.

"That's what I needed to see," he said. "They're settin' up camp." He then swung the pickup around and headed back to Highway 97. At a phone booth in Weed, he made a call to Fish and Game dispatch and passed on the information. The fate of the antelope poacher now lay in other hands.

Sunrise two mornings later found Taylor in waders, thigh-deep in the Klamath River, doing what he liked best. His nine-foot fly rod cut graceful arcs through the chill air as he false-casted, feeding line through the guides, doublehauling, and finally shooting the weighted line across the dancing waters of Skunk Riffle. The line turned nicely, and the #8 Brindle Bug gently touched the surface and went under.

Taylor mended line as the fly was swept downstream. At the end of the drift, as the fly swung cross-current, it caught the eye of a sleek, rainbow-striped steelhead, fresh from the sea. The fish reacted instantly, slamming the fly hard. Taylor struck back with the rod-tip, and four pounds of silver-scaled lightning took to the air. Twice in five seconds the fish leaped and thrashed, then it streaked upstream, the line hissing through the dark water. It jumped again at the end of the run, then shot down river. Ten minutes later, the exhausted fish lay on its side in the sunlit shallows. Taylor regarded it with genuine affection as he gently removed the hook. He then walked it to deeper water and released it.

It was his eighth fish of the trip, having caught and released seven the day before. Klamath River steelhead weren't large, but they were numerous. And they were renowned scrappers. Most of the fish were under three pounds and were referred to collectively as half-pounders. Taylor had learned to love this fishing as a student at Humboldt State, and he returned each year, whenever he had the chance.

He and Nancy liked to camp at the Dillon Creek Campground, about 10 miles below Happy Camp. And it was here, two days earlier, that they had come after dealing with the antelope poacher. The family was still unaware of the results of their efforts concerning the poacher, but they would later learn that a warden had acted on the information and had not only captured the poacher in the field with an illegally tagged antelope, but had verified that the man had submitted no fewer than eight bogus tag applications for the current year.

Following his release of the four-pound fish, Taylor waded back to the gravel bar where he had left his rubber raft. Nancy had dropped him off with the raft at first light so that he could fish and float the two miles back to camp at his leisure. The raft provided him the means to access both sides of the river, plus a handy way to get from riffle to riffle. He now walked the raft into knee-deep water and gingerly climbed aboard, careful to avoid puncturing the raft with his spike-soled wading sandals. As he was fitting the oars in the raft's oarlocks, the boom of a rifle shot brought him up short. He turned to look downstream, estimating that the shooter had to be at least a mile away. Reminding himself he was on vacation, he rowed to the next riffle and resumed fishing.

Midmorning found him again in the raft, again floating from one riffle to the next. As he drifted along in silence, movement downstream on the south bank caught his attention. As he drew nearer, he could make out two men who appeared to be dragging a large dark object along a trail that skirted the river. *Could that be a bear?* he wondered. Drawing nearer still, he concluded that the object was indeed a medium-size bear.

Being 99 percent certain that bear season had not yet opened in the area, he assessed his options and decided to shadow the two men and learn whatever he could. Stopping at a gravel bar about 150 yards upstream from the men, he stepped out with his fly rod and began casting. Soon they spotted him. Watching from the corner of his eye, he could immediately tell from their reaction that they were uncomfortable with his presence and indeed were up to no good. He noted also that at least one of them was armed with a rifle.

Continuing to cast and continuing to watch, Taylor correctly concluded that the suspects needed to cross the river. Not only was the highway on the opposite side from them, but there was a cabin and outbuildings with which Taylor had a hunch they were associated. After staring at him for a while, apparently in discussion, they finally stepped into some brush and reappeared dragging a rubber raft, much like Taylor's, but larger. They launched the raft and with no small difficulty wrestled the bear into it. They then climbed in, pushed off and paddled for the opposite bank.

Taylor watched until they landed near the cabin and dragged the bear someplace out of his view. He then climbed into his own raft and he, too, crossed to the highway side. He stashed his raft and fishing gear, then headed down river, keeping to the brush. He crept to within a stone's throw of the cabin, and with the utmost care he was able to get a look at the grounds and outbuildings. A dark blue Chevy Suburban and a battered, older Ford pickup were parked there. Neither the suspects nor the bear were in sight.

Having gleaned all the information he could, it was now time to get some help. Creeping back upstream a safe distance, he hiked up to the highway and flagged down a man in a pickup.

"I'm a game warden, and I need a ride into town," said Taylor.

"Climb in," said the man. They hadn't gone far when they spotted a California Highway Patrol unit coming their way. They were able to flag it down, and with the CHP officer's help, Taylor was soon in touch with Warden Frank Cox of Happy Camp. Cox was well aware of the cabin Taylor described, having once arrested its owner, Robert Passmore, for gillnetting and a variety of lesser offenses. But in view of Taylor's description of the suspects, even though obtained from considerable distance, Cox felt certain that neither of the suspects was Passmore.

Shortly before noon, Cox drove Taylor in the patrol vehicle to a turnout about a quarter mile from the cabin. Taylor, carrying a handset radio, slipped out of the passenger side and disappeared into the brush. Cox stayed with the patrol vehicle while Taylor again crept close to the cabin. Nothing had changed. He worked his way to the rear of the cabin, and when he had a clear view of everything not visible from the front, he whispered into the radio. Thirty seconds later Cox pulled down the driveway in the patrol vehicle and parked in front of the cabin. The wardens had agreed that Taylor would stay out of sight unless necessity dictated otherwise, for it would have complicated his future fishing trips and perhaps endangered his family had the locals known him to be a warden.

"HEY, BOB," shouted Cox. "I NEED TO TALK TO YOU." The front door creaked open and Robert Passmore appeared. The man stood no more than five-foot-four, his face a bag of sad eyes and wrinkles. "I need to talk to your friends about the bear," Cox announced.

"What bear?" said Passmore.

"Don't play games with me, Bob, unless you want in on this yourself," said Cox.

Passmore brooded over his predicament for a few seconds, then turned toward the cabin and called out, "You guys better come out here." There came a whisper of conversation inside the cabin, then the door again opened and a much younger man appeared.

"I'm the one you want," he said. "I killed the bear."

"What about the other guy?" Cox inquired.

"He didn't have nothin' to do with it. I'm the one that shot it." He then identified himself as Albert Worley, a resident of the Bay Area. Cox, in a particularly good mood, decided to let the other guy off.

Passmore led Cox into a room that smelled like a dumpster. The bear carcass was there on a table, skinned and hacked into quarters. Worley helped Cox lug the quarters and the hide out to the patrol vehicle.

"Hey, man, I live in San Francisco," said Worley. "I don't want to come all the way back here to take care of this. Is there any way I can do it today?"

As it happened, there was a way. A half hour later, he found himself at the Happy Camp courthouse, face to face with the toughest judge in four counties. Cox had taken him forthwith, as they say. The judge accepted the man's guilty plea, fixed him with a withering gaze, then promptly fined him about half a month's pay.

———————

It had not been the best of vacations for the Taylors. Nor had it been the worst. Unwelcome rain, off and on, had kept Nancy cooped up in the tent with the boys while Taylor, oblivious to weather while pursuing steelhead, had fished. The boys, however, had not been a problem, having spent many of the stormy hours tying flies by lantern light, a skill taught to them by their father. And Nancy had found the sound of raindrops on canvas somehow pleasant and relaxing. When sunshine had prevailed, the boys, too young yet to safely fish the Klamath, had taken their share of small rainbows and browns in Dillon Creek, casting flies of their own manufacture. And they had captured a variety of frogs and salamanders for close examination as well.

Taylor felt a bit guilty as he stuffed the last of their camping gear into the camper shell. It was time to go, and he had again subjected his vacationing family to Fish and Game business. But for him there was little choice. He was a game warden, through and through, his mission to protect wildlife. And he found it impossible to set this mission aside.

But Nancy and the boys didn't seem particularly unhappy, he thought, as they busied themselves with one final policing of their campsite. The boys, in fact, were downright merry, glancing often across the campground to where a uniformed game warden was issuing a citation. The recipient of the citation, his face a mask of grim resignation, was a game hog. Or, more accurately, a fish hog. He had been one for years, having little regard for bag limits. Because he was a careful violator, he had not until now been caught. But now it was time to pay the fiddler.

The violator was what the wardens referred to as a "multiple tripper." His thing was to catch a limit of fish, take them back to camp, then return to the river for more. During this latest stay on the river he had taken multiple limits of half-pounders each day, storing them in ice chests. But this time he had come to grief. *How had it happened?* he wondered. He had been so careful, so discreet, so totally cunning. But he had made one tiny mistake, failed to notice one seemingly insignificant factor . . . the scrutiny of two freckle-faced boys.

ROOKIE

It began with the midnight theft of a boat. The thieves, two of them in dark clothing, spotted the 14-foot aluminum Valco, the property of a local lifeguard, chained to a metal post near the beach. They applied bolt cutters to the chain which parted with a barely audible snick. Two minutes later, they had the boat and its pair of oars in the bed of a small pickup and were gone.

Night Patrol. Warden Mark Lucero, Department of Fish and Game, was ready for anything. He drove south along Camino de la Costa, his sharp eyes probing the darkness. To his right, beyond the rock-studded La Jolla shoreline, the Pacific Ocean lay calm and placid in the moonlight. It was an hour past midnight when he passed two men in a small gray pickup. Lashed to the back of the vehicle was an aluminum boat.

Lucero was a rookie. But he was a talented rookie, and during his first year on the job he had done much to distinguish himself. He had a good eye for warden work.

Good instincts. It was therefore not surprising that with only a brief glance at the two men in the pickup, he recognized them for exactly what they were—outlaws on the prowl.

He passed them in an area where high-dollar homes lined wide streets with names like Avenida de Cortez and Calle de los Robles. His patrol vehicle was a fully equipped, dark green pickup with emergency lights on the cab and Fish and Game's logo emblazoned on its doors, and yet the two men were so intent on studying the beach that they failed to recognize him. They drove right by him, unaware.

The beach at this point, Windansea Beach, was but a 200-yard-long strip of sand, a break in an otherwise rugged, rocky stretch of coastline jutting out into the Pacific. It was an area fished heavily by commercial lobster fishermen who set their buoy-marked traps in close, just beyond the breakers. Because the multi-colored buoys were in plain sight from shore, and because lobsters were such a valuable commodity, thievery was a problem here. Well aware of this, Lucero reached for his radio microphone and made a call. Warden Mike Castleton, a few miles to the south, answered immediately. A few minutes later the two wardens met, and Lucero hurriedly advised Castleton of what he had seen.

"I've got a hunch they're gonna rob lobster traps," said Lucero. "I'd bet on it."

Castleton, who had been the last of Lucero's three field training officers a few months earlier, had learned that Lucero's hunches deserved serious consideration.

"Let's go find' em," said Castleton. They quickly devised a search plan and headed back to the area near Windansea Beach.

It was Lucero who again spotted the gray pickup, parked about where he expected it to be. He called in Castleton, and from cover, about 60 yards from the parked pickup, they watched as the two men unloaded the boat. But they were assisted now by a third man who had arrived in a small car. They had chosen to park on a side street, a couple of houses up from Camino de la Costa, beyond which was the beach. After the third man put a large container into the boat, they picked up the boat and headed off with it. They lugged it to the corner, then crossed Camino de la Costa to the beach where they vanished in the darkness.

The wardens now crept closer to the parked vehicles, attempting to get the license numbers. They failed, however, due to the immediate return of one of the three suspects. They had to dive for cover. Unaware of their presence, the returning suspect slipped into the small compact and drove away. Lucero was able to get only a partial plate number.

The wardens now made a quick battle plan. Castleton would sneak out onto the beach and attempt to see the outlaws in action. Lucero would remain with the pickup to prevent the escape of the outlaws should they get by Castleton.

As Castleton hurried away, Lucero picked a spot in some shrubbery near the pickup and made himself comfortable. As he settled down to wait, his right hand strayed to his badge, the six-pointed star of silver and gold over his heart. It was but a small thing, and yet he was immensely proud of it, and he reveled again in the wondrous certainty that he was at last doing exactly what he wanted to do with his life.

His thoughts wandered back over the year of remarkable events that had brought him to the present. He had not originally set out to become a game warden. The idea had struck him rather recently. He had earned a degree in broadcast journalism and had held a good job as video news editor at Channel 10 News in Sacramento. But he grew restless, dissatisfied with totally indoor work. He returned to college and earned a second degree in natural science, envisioning himself as a State Park ranger. Somewhere along the line, however, he decided to take the Fish and Game warden exam. He now regarded this decision as perhaps the best of his life. He excelled on the exam and landed one of the few openings available. And his first look at warden work was love at first sight.

A mere three days following his graduation from the San Diego Sheriff's Academy, he faced his first armed outlaws. He and Lt. Art Lawrence, on night patrol, had braced a pair of drug-high, would-be deer poachers. A Fish and Game pilot, high above, had sighted the poachers spotlighting, and Lucero and Lawrence were first to make contact. The vehicle they were after, a pickup, was stopped when they found it. One man stood in its bed, apparently tossing out rubbish, and a second man stood behind its tailgate, holding a rifle at port arms.

"FISH AND GAME!" shouted Lawrence from behind his open door. "PUT THE GUN DOWN!" But the man failed to comply. "PUT THE GUN DOWN!" Lawrence shouted, drawing his sidearm, but still the man clung to the rifle. At this moment, brand new Warden Mark Lucero, who had exited the patrol vehicle with the 12 gage riot shotgun, applied a bit of training he had learned only two weeks earlier at the academy. He jacked a round into the chamber of the shotgun, producing the loud and ominous CLACK CLACK sound guaranteed to freeze the blood of most criminals, and shouted.

"PUT THE GUN DOWN OR YOU WILL BE SHOT!"

The outlaw threw down the rifle as though it were on fire. From this moment on, Art Lawrence regarded his new trainee in a different light.

Adventure had followed adventure, and Lucero had thrived on it. There were enjoyable weeks spent in the southeast corner of the state with Warden Rusty McBride, known far and wide as the Yuma Puma. McBride, a genuine desert rat, was a highly experienced, highly skilled warden from whom Lucero learned plenty. Lucero came away from the experience with some memorable moments as well.

One such moment occurred during a January jet-boat patrol on the Colorado River. As they were skimming along at exhilarating speed, McBride at the controls and Lucero poised in the bow like Washington crossing the Delaware, they struck a hidden sand bar. The boat and the Yuma Puma came to an abrupt stop. Lucero, however, continued on. Airborne for at least 20 feet, he executed a perfect tuck and roll, struck the ankle-deep water with a monstrous splash, and miraculously rolled to his feet. When it was apparent that he was all in one piece, both men broke into laughter. They laughed, in fact, until they could no longer stand.

"If you keep jumpin' out of the boat," gasped McBride, "I'll flunk you on your probation." More laughter.

McBride again demonstrated his capacity for humor a week later at Andrade, a port of entry between California and Mexico. He and Lucero were checking for overlimits of pheasants and waterfowl being smuggled in from Mexico, a not-uncommon practice. Among the people they checked on this day were a Hispanic man, woman and tiny child with fishing equipment and some freshly caught fish. They, however, had no fishing licenses for either Mexico or California and could therefore not legally possess the fish. Upon determining that they could not speak English, McBride, well aware that Lucero was bilingual, turned to him and spoke.

"Pay attention, Lucero. You're about to hear some real Spanish." He then addressed the people in a crude version of their native tongue. Because he had decided to let them off with a warning, he attempted to tell them that he would assume that the baby had caught the fish. He then added that he would have to take the fish. Due, however, to some imperfections in his delivery, he somehow convinced the woman that he intended to take her child. She shrank back in horror, clutching the child protectively.

"Mi bebe?" she cried, "Que paso con mi bebe?"

McBride stood puzzled over this unexpected reaction, but Lucero smoothly intervened. He soon set the misunderstanding right and sent the people on their way. Even then, however, the woman cast a suspicious eye over her shoulder at McBride as they departed. Undaunted, McBride faced Lucero, struck a cocky pose, his thumbs hooked in his belt, grinned broadly and said, "Not bad, huh?"

Lucero smiled at the memory, then recalled another incident which had provided him a lesson in the incredible strength of animals. Acting on a tip, he and Warden Mike Fitzsimmons had driven to a home in South San Diego where a resident was reported to be keeping an illegally imported monkey. They were greeted there by the suspect, a skinny, shaggy-haired young man with an ugly festering wound on his right forearm. Fitzsimmons explained why he and Lucero were there, then inquired about the wound. "The monkey bit me," said the man. "He hates people."

The man then opened his garage and pointed to a portable cage in which sat a spider monkey of about 40 pounds. It sat quietly, mid-cage, appearing quite docile. But he watched their every move with eyes that never blinked.

"Let's get it to the truck," said Fitzsimmons, and as they bent to pick up the cage, the monkey made its move. With astounding quickness, the animal sprang at Lucero, shot its arm through the wire, grabbed a fist-full of the warden's hair and yanked his head hard against the cage. Lucero then glimpsed wicked-looking incisors flashing toward his face, and he jerked free just barely in time.

"That's one mean monkey!" he said, smoothing down his hair. And as if to substantiate this statement, the monkey now went for Fitzsimmons' gun. The little hand shot out, locked onto the pistol butt and nearly tugged Fitzsimmons off his feet. With remarkable presence of mind, Fitzsimmons simply gave the monkey's hand a sharp slap. The monkey jerked back its hand and pouted like a chastised child.

"Think of it, Fitz," said Lucero later. "You could've been gunned down by a monkey!"

Lucero was chuckling to himself over the memory when a radio call brought him back to the present. It was Castleton.

"They're back on the beach," he said. "They just scuttled the boat in the surf."

Lucero readied himself while Castleton attempted to keep an eye on the suspects. But the suspects didn't head directly back to their pickup. Castleton could see them struggling up the beach with something heavy between them, but then he lost them in the poor light. Moving carefully and staying low, he attempted to catch up with them, but they had vanished.

Soon thereafter, Lucero saw the suspects coming. But they were empty-handed. Upon arriving at the pickup they began to change clothes. They both were wearing dark-colored pullover sweatshirts, and both began pulling the garments over their heads at the same time. While their hands and arms were temporarily restricted, Lucero stepped into view.

"State Game Wardens," he said.

There was no sign of surprise by the suspects. They didn't jump, they didn't spin around, they didn't speak. They simply froze. And to Lucero, there could have been no more ominous a reaction. Hairs prickled on the back of his neck as he correctly sensed he was in the presence of veteran criminals. His right thumb sought the safety snap on his holster.

"Why are you guys all wet?" said Lucero.

There was a long pause before one of them finally answered. "We were wrestling down on the beach and fell into the ocean," he said.

"I see," said Lucero. "What happened to your boat?"

"Boat? We don't have no boat," said the same man. "But we just saw some divers walking down the beach. Maybe it was theirs."

Lucero then asked the two men to move to the front of their pickup where they were more directly illuminated by a nearby street light.

"Now, would you mind holding up your hands and turning around slowly for me?" he said. "Good. Do you have any weapons? Any guns or knives?"

They were apparently unarmed, but Lucero at no time let his guard down. He separated the two men a few feet, then moved in and handcuffed one of them.

"What's this all about?" the man inquired.

"We think you might be stealing lobsters," said Lucero. "Let's take a walk." Shadowing them from behind, he directed them across the street and onto the beach. Castleton met them there and immediately handcuffed the second suspect. He then headed them for the hidden patrol vehicles while Lucero went in search of the stash of lobsters that was certain to be nearby.

Casting his flashlight beam across the beach, Lucero soon spotted the abandoned boat, overturned, waves still pounding it. Then he saw tracks and drag marks that led inland. The tracks led to a trail which in turn led him to a small dumpster and some trash cans. One of the trash cans was wet. Lifting the lid of the wet one, he found it to be nearly full of lobsters, most of them under legal size. He gave a low whistle. In with the lobsters was an object that puzzled him—a single swim fin of unusual make.

After informing Castleton of his find, Lucero trotted across Camino de la Costa to the suspects' gray pickup. Casting his flashlight beam into the open bed of the vehicle he found wet clothing, including two sets of wet gloves, and an additional object that made him smile. It was a single swim fin of unusual make, a perfect match to the one he had found with the lobsters.

It was all over but the paperwork. Lucero ran thorough records checks on the suspects, and despite the fact that both men had lengthy rap sheets, there were no current arrest warrants out for them. For a number of reasons, the wardens decided to release the suspects and file charges on them later. Time would be helpful in determining what exactly to charge the two with. There was the matter of the boat to consider. It was most likely freshly stolen, for it had not yet been reported and was therefore not yet in the computer. So, the lobster pirates were cut free. But time would prove their freedom to be short-lived.

Dawn found the wardens wrestling the abandoned boat to high ground to be examined and photographed. They had already processed the other evidence. The trash can, they found, contained 88 spiny lobsters, 77 of which were undersize "shorts."

With the investigation complete, the wardens prepared to part company. As Castleton wearily approached his patrol vehicle he paused and turned to face Lucero.

"Good job, Mark!" he said. "Really great case!"

Lucero smiled and waved acknowledgement, gestures that failed to reflect the warm glow that washed over his heart. He had quickly learned, during his first year, that the business of protecting wildlife provided a variety of fine rewards, not the least of which was honest praise from a warden of the caliber of Mike Castleton.

As Lucero headed for home that day, he thought back over his relationship with Castleton, the man who had become his mentor and later one of his closest friends. Lucero then chuckled to himself as he recalled an incident that had occurred a few months earlier. He and Castleton had assisted Warden Mike Fitzsimmons at Mission Bay in checking a returning party boat full of anglers. Castleton was delayed at the parking lot and Lucero joined Fitzsimmons on the dock as the boat pulled in. Fitzsimmons immediately hopped aboard and approached the boat's skipper in the wheelhouse. Lucero remained near the gangway to check the anglers as they came ashore with their catches.

There were perhaps a dozen returning anglers, and Lucero checked them, one by one, examining fishing licenses and fish in wet burlap sacks. But he immediately noticed that two of the anglers, two men, appeared to be nervous or agitated and were reluctant to come ashore. They were further noteworthy in that they were two of the largest human beings Lucero had ever seen. Their combined weight, the warden judged, would top 600 pounds, and they obviously spent most of their waking hours pumping iron. They had no visible necks, their bald-shorn heads apparently joined directly to huge bodies, and their monstrously muscled arms and tree-trunk legs stood Lucero in awe. When they alone remained aboard, Lucero addressed them.

"Gentlemen, I'll need to talk to you as well."

They eyed him with undisguised malice and finally lumbered down the gangway. Lucero had seen friendlier eyes on rattlesnakes.

"May I see your fishing licenses, please?" said Lucero.

"We don't have licenses," said one, his voice a rumbling bass. "The captain said we didn't need 'em. Now, you step aside, 'cause we're leavin'."

They started to barge around him on the narrow dock, but he moved and blocked their path. "I'm sorry, gentlemen, but you definitely need fishing licenses," he said. "Now, I'll need to see your identification."

"What if we refuse? What are you gonna do about it?" growled one of them.

"I'll have to take you to jail," said Lucero.

"HEY, SKIPPER, YOU BETTER GET DOWN HERE!" one of them shouted in the direction of the boat's wheelhouse. But the skipper, who had failed to fill out his logs, was arguing with Warden Fitzsimmons. The owner of the landing, however, was nearby and heard the shouting. He rushed from his little office on the pier and strode angrily toward Lucero. But Castleton had by now arrived, and he intercepted the man and sat him down on the dock.

Meanwhile, to Lucero's amazement, the two monster-men appeared to go crazy—Hulk Hogan style. With bared teeth, they began stomping their feet, growling, and flexing their enormous muscles threateningly.

"AARRRRRRR! URRRRRRRR!"

But Lucero, even though his death or dismemberment appeared imminent, stood his ground. Finally, the monster-men appeared to lose their steam, and ultimately they stood sullenly as Lucero issued them each a citation. Clinton K. McNabb went first.

"What's your occupation, Mr. McNabb?" Lucero asked, upon reaching this box on the citation.

"We're wrestlers," said McNabb. Then his eyes narrowed, and he thrust his face closer to the warden. "Do you have a problem with that?"

"No sir, no problem at all," answered Lucero quickly.

When Lucero completed the citation, he handed it to McNabb to sign. McNabb snatched the pen from Lucero and signed "Killer McNabb" in the appropriate box. Upon seeing Lucero about to question this, his eyes narrowed again, and again he leaned closer to the warden.

"It's my name. That's how people know me. Do you have a problem with that?" he growled.

Lucero considered the matter briefly, then answered, "No sir, no problem at all."

Without further incident, Lucero finished his business with the monster-men, grateful to have survived the experience.

That night after work, when Lucero was home and just finishing dinner, the phone rang. It was Mike Castleton, highly amused over something.

"Go turn on Channel 2," said Castleton.

Lucero carried his cordless phone into the living room and turned on the TV to Channel 2. It was a ring-side view of a wrestling match at the San Diego Sports Arena, and there, big as life, was Killer McNabb in the act of destroying his opponent. As Lucero watched, McNabb effortlessly picked up his dazed opponent, spun him around a few times and slammed him to the mat. There the man remained, apparently unable to rise. McNabb then climbed leisurely to the top of the turn-buckled ropes in one corner, stood poised for a second and then launched himself. He appeared to land fanny-first, square in the middle of his prostrate victim.

"Look at that!" said Castleton. "That could've been you!"

"You're right," said Lucero with conviction. "That *definitely* could've been me."

GRAND TRICKERY

John Baisley awoke suddenly, his eyes fixing on patterns of light creeping along the walls and ceiling of his bedroom. Then the low grind of tires on gravel came to his ears. Oregon Gulch Road was infrequently traveled, even during daylight, so the slow passing of a vehicle near to midnight was cause for suspicion.

Baisley rolled out of bed, padded to a window and peered out into the night. His mobile home, perched as it was on a ridge, provided an excellent view of the surrounding countryside. The Feather River, a half mile below, was invisible in the darkness, but the lights of Oroville twinkled beyond. Baisley spotted the approaching headlights, then a stab of light from the right side of the vehicle. Someone within had directed a powerful spotlight across the slope above the road.

"What is it, John?" Nora Baisley was now awake.

"Don't know," said Baisley. "Maybe deer poachers."

He watched the vehicle pass his gate, the driver having apparently increased speed upon sighting the residence. The spotlight was now switched off, but it came on again soon thereafter. Baisley could see the bright beam playing across the oak and Digger pine slopes and the open meadows. The vehicle continued its twisting path along the mountainside until it was out of sight, but Baisley could still glimpse the spotlight beam at work. Then the light appeared to steady on something well out of his view, and seconds later a rifle shot boomed from that direction. Baisley turned and headed for the phone.

Whatever dreams were playing through the sleep-numbed brain of Lt. James Halber shattered instantly upon the first harsh ring of the telephone. Groping for the receiver in the darkness, he picked it up and answered.

"This is John Baisley, up on Oregon Gulch Road. I think someone just shot a deer up here."

Baisley, Halber thought, searching his memory, *Oregon Gulch Road.* Then it dawned on him. He had met the man a month earlier, left him a business card and solicited his help.

"You said to call day or night," Baisley continued, "so I took you at your word." Halber thanked him and pressed him for details concerning the poachers.

"I think they shot somewhere near where the big power lines cross the road," said Baisley. "And I think they're in a small pickup. They were headed toward town."

Halber again thanked the man and promised to be there shortly. Six minutes later, after splashing cold water on his face, leaping into a uniform and strapping on his gun belt, he rolled out of his driveway in his big Dodge patrol truck. Leaving Oroville, he sped across the Feather River Bridge then north on Cherokee Road, ascending higher into the foothills of the Sierra Nevada. He turned east onto Oregon Gulch Road and snapped off his headlights. Darkness enveloped him. Then he flipped a small switch under his dash and he could see again—but just barely. The tiny glow cast by the "sneak light" on his front bumper was enough to drive by, but no more. It would, however, ensure that he would detect an approaching vehicle before its occupants spotted *him,* thereby providing him a few valuable seconds to prepare for the stop.

And so it happened. Halber had gone less than a half mile when headlights appeared. Instantly he hit the kill switch to the sneak light and slid to a stop. He waited in darkness until the approaching headlights were about to fall on him, then he snapped on his own bright lights and his red emergency light. The startled driver of the other vehicle instinctively hit the brakes. Halber pulled in front of him, blocking his path, making a head-on stop.

Halber hesitated just long enough to train the beam of his roof-mounted spotlight into the face of the other driver, then he was out the door, flashlight in hand. He made a quick but cautious approach to the open passenger window of the vehicle. It was a small blue pickup with camping gear in back, and the driver was alone. Directing his flashlight inside the cab, Halber knew instantly that he had the right vehicle. One look at the driver was enough— a terrified man trying to look otherwise.

"You're a slow learner, Randy," said Halber. Randy Lysec, age 26, was a local outlaw whom Halber had dealt with before and whose older brother he'd tangled with before that. The older brother, in fact, was serving a life sentence for beating a man to death with a claw hammer.

The reason for Randy Lysec's terror, or at least *part* of the reason, was apparent, for leaning butts-down against the passenger side of the front seat were three big-game rifles. And still plugged into the cigarette lighter on the dash was a powerful, Q-beam spotlight.

"Turn off the engine," said Halber. "I'm gonna have to check your rifles." Lysec complied. Halber opened the passenger door and slid the bolt back on each of the rifles. Two were empty, but the third held a fired casing in the chamber. Halber sniffed the open end of the cartridge case, then the bore of the rifle. The stench of freshly fired powder in both was still strong.

"What did you shoot?" Halber demanded.

"I shot at a coyote," said Lysec, gripping the wheel to quell the shaking of his hands.

Unlike his brother, Randy Lysec was not a tough guy. He could not meet Halber's eyes, and Halber sensed correctly that the man could be intimidated. The warden therefore set about using this weakness against him.

"Don't give me that," said Halber, fixing Lysec with a withering gaze. "I know *exactly* what you were doing, and you're real lucky you missed. And I'll tell you something else . . . ."

Halber's voice now gained volume and intensity, and he aimed his index finger like a gun barrel at the man's face.

"I'm gonna make it my personal business to catch you the next time you try this. Now you'd better go home."

Lysec didn't linger, and Halber couldn't help being amused by the man's dilemma as he drove away. The evidence in Lysec's pickup told a clear story. Halber was certain that two other suspects had been with Lysec. They had undoubtedly spotlighted and killed a deer, and the other two were now out field dressing the deer.

Lysec faced the problem of how to return and pick up his friends without again encountering Halber. Halber figured that Lysec would wait an hour or two, then drive in to rescue his friends. Halber intended to ambush them as they returned to town, a package deal. Hopefully, they would have fresh deer blood on them, for in light of Lysec's recent scare, Halber rated the chances of them bringing out the deer as slim to none.

But Halber faced a problem. There were two ways into the Oregon Gulch area, and Halber could watch but one. Reaching for his radio microphone, he called dispatch. Soon thereafter, Warden Fred Brown, not yet fully awake, made a hurried departure from his home in Gridley. Racing up Highway 70, he would take up a position at the north end of Cherokee Road, while Halber guarded the south end.

In the meantime, Halber continued up Oregon Gulch Road to the Baisley place. With no further need for stealth, he now traveled with his high-beams. As he passed the sweeping turn beneath the giant power lines, he swept the area with his roof-mounted spotlight. Nothing. Upon reaching Baisley's gate, he tapped on the horn, and Baisley soon appeared. Baisley again recounted what he had seen and heard, this time pointing out where things had happened.

"I know there were at least two people in the pickup, maybe three," he continued. Halber again thanked him, turned the patrol truck around and headed back to the power lines.

With practiced strokes of a keen-bladed sheath knife, Bradley Pane, bloody to the elbows, labored in the waning moonlight, field dressing a four-point buck. Assisting with this task was his friend, Clinton Clabo, grasping one of the buck's hind legs and nervously studying the gravel road. The road passed a hundred yards below them down the none-too-gentle slope. Overhead, high-voltage electricity surged through metal cables strung from tower to tower down the mountainside.

When headlights appeared, both men ducked low and were glad that they had taken the time to drag the dead deer into a depression behind one of several granite outcroppings on the slope. And they were *really* glad they had done so when the approaching vehicle appeared and its roof-mounted spotlight came to life and began sweeping the slope. They remained hidden until the vehicle was well around a bend and gone.

"Do you think it was a warden?" Clabo asked.

"I don't know," said Pane. "But it sure wasn't *Randy!*"

Following a brief discussion, they decided to stick with their plan. But five minutes later they were regretting this decision. Not only did the same vehicle return, but this time it stopped, its spotlight now stationary, illuminating the slope. Venturing a peek, Clabo was horrified to see a figure bearing a flashlight emerge from the vehicle and start up the slope toward them.

"Stay low and don't move," whispered Pane urgently.

Lieutenant Halber didn't really expect to find anything as he hiked up the slope, searching with his flashlight. But he knew it would be good for him to make a show of searching and then giving up. The bad guys were probably watching his every move, but even if he stumbled onto them, the best he could hope for would be a foot chase that he could easily lose. Better to wait until he could stop them in a vehicle, far from the deer, when they felt less threatened.

Halber searched up one side of the slope, then down the other, unaware when he passed within 30 yards of the two terrified poachers and the downed buck. Had he continued up the slope another 20 feet he would have spotted the drag marks in the damp grass. But having seen nothing, he returned to his patrol vehicle and headed back toward Oroville.

Pane and Clabo, having experienced a very narrow escape, forgot about the deer and headed north across country. Fortunately for them, and bad luck for Halber, Clabo had relatives living at an isolated ranch within an hour's walk. The outlaws had in fact planned to make their way there should something go wrong. Lysec had been instructed to simply leave the area if he encountered game wardens.

But Halber, with no knowledge of any of this, proceeded with the most appropriate action based on what he knew. He waited. He chose a hidden spot along Cherokee Road and waited for Lysec to return to pick up his friends. Ten miles to the north, Warden Fred Brown lay in ambush on the opposite end of the road. The wardens were prepared for anything, fully expecting Lysec to use another vehicle or some other trick. But nothing happened.

After three hours of fruitless waiting, Halber decided to call it off. He reached for his mike and called Brown.

"I guess we'd better give it up. Sorry to call you out on a wild goose chase," said Halber.

"That's okay," said Brown. "This'll make up for the last one I called you out on."

Halber fired his engine and headed wearily back for Oregon Gulch Road. Not yet ready to admit defeat, he would search again for the deer. He was *certain* they had killed one. But even if it was still there and he found it, he knew that Lysec would simply deny all knowledge of it. Halber had to admit that his chances of success on this case were growing dim.

He had just turned onto Oregon Gulch Road when the idea struck him. He braked to a stop as he warmed to the thought. Could it work? It would be a long-shot, trickery on a grand scale. But even if it failed, the idea of rousting Randy Lysec out of bed at 3:30 a.m. held definite appeal. Halber chuckled to himself as he spun the patrol truck around and again headed for Oroville. He was almost cheerful as he rumbled across the Feather River Bridge and continued south toward the old part of town.

Lysec's place was one-half of a ramshackle duplex. The fenced yard contained an abandoned refrigerator, a wrecked car and a pit bull, the residence a sad blight to an otherwise pleasant, tree-shaded street. Halber, having been there before, ignored the furious barking and false charges of the dog as he strode to the front door. Glancing at the dog, he thought, *I hope my bluff works better than yours.*

BOOM BOOM BOOM, Halber hammered on the door. The dog barked. A half minute passed. BOOM BOOM BOOM. Finally the door opened, and there stood a bleary-eyed, terrified Randy Lysec.

"Well, I guess you know why I'm here," said Halber, fixing Lysec with a stern gaze. Lysec hung his head and stared at his bare feet. "What do you have to say for yourself?" Halber continued. But before Lysec could answer, a tousle-haired little woman appeared, bundled in a pink robe.

"Is he gonna be able to come home tonight?" she asked.

"I don't know, ma'am. We'll have to go pick up the deer first, then talk to the other guys." The woman now stared at *her* feet.

"Randy, you'd better get dressed," said Halber, and he almost held his breath during the two minutes it took Lysec to pull on shirt and shoes.

"What's this gonna cost us?" the woman inquired.

"I don't know, ma'am. That'll be up to the judge," said Halber. Then Lysec was ready, and without a word from Halber, the man walked out and climbed into the patrol truck. "Put your seatbelt on," said Halber.

During the drive back up to Oregon Gulch Road, Halber got Lysec talking about events long past, non-threatening things, and as the man talked, his fear rapidly diminished. This worried Halber, but he had to keep the man talking. He couldn't allow him time to ponder his present predicament.

"Do you remember the time you caught my brother and me pitchforking salmon?" said Lysec.

"I remember," said Halber. "You must've been about 15 then. And I *also* remember catching you with a boned-out deer in a suitcase."

"That wasn't me. That was my brother. He used to go after 'em with his car." Halber could remember the car, a big sedan. It had looked exactly like one would expect a car to look after a dozen or more intentional collisions with deer.

Upon turning onto Oregon Gulch Road, Halber's tension grew, but Lysec babbled on. When they neared the power lines, Halber slowed the patrol vehicle and leaned forward to peer out the windshield as though searching for a reference point.

"Up a ways," said Lysec, and Halber speeded up a bit. "Here," said Lysec, and Halber braked to a stop.

As Lysec unbuckled his seatbelt, Halber handed him a small flashlight. Because Halber had no idea which way to go from the patrol vehicle, he was greatly relieved when Lysec stepped out and immediately crossed in front of him and started up the slope. Halber followed him. Lysec stopped once to get his bearings, then led Halber directly to the rock outcropping. Halber stepped around it and there lay the buck beside a pile of entrails. Only then was the warden able to breathe normally again.

In taking Halber to the deer, Lysec had demonstrated his involvement in the crime, unknowingly providing Halber with the evidence that would lead to his conviction. Halber now had a poacher-killed deer and a poacher to go with it. But he knew that the *real* culprits had yet to be caught.

"Grab a hold," said Halber, taking one side of the wide antlers. Lysec took the other side, and together they made short work of dragging the buck down the slope to the patrol truck. Halber dropped the tailgate, and they hefted the animal up and into the bed. Halber then used his folding knife to cut a deep but narrow slit in the heavy muscles of one of the deer's hams. Into this slit, he inserted a thermometer. The temperature of the carcass would confirm that the animal had been killed at night, a bit of evidence Halber could well need.

As he worked, Halber's mind raced. It appeared that Lysec had assumed, as Halber had intended, that his companions had already been caught. It was an edge Halber now set about exploiting.

"I thought you were *over* this kind of stuff," said Halber. "How'd you get mixed up with those guys?"

"Well, I grew up with Brad, and Clint's married to my sister," said Lysec. "They're not that bad."

Halber shook his head sadly as he opened his citation book and began to write. After asking Lysec a string of non-threatening questions, putting him even more at ease, he hit him with, "How does Brad spell his last name? Does it have an E in it?"

"Yeah. It's P . . . A . . . N . . . E," said Lysec. Halber almost felt guilty. *Bradley John Pane,* another of his old customers.

Halber now had one of the two missing suspects, and he was certain that an inquiry at Oroville Police Department would provide him the other. Oroville cops were experts on the Lysec family, and they would undoubtedly know not only which Clint in town had married one of the Lysec girls, but where the two lived. But still, Halber thought, it wouldn't hurt to try.

"How does Clint spell *his* name?" he asked. Lysec started to answer, then suspicion, long overdue, suddenly flashed in his eyes. Halber turned instantly to glare at him and demand, "This ain't the time to jack me around, Randy, now how do you spell his name."

"C . . . L . . . A . . . B . . . O."

A half hour later, Halber stood at Clinton Clabo's door, a bit surprised to find that the man had successfully made his way home. Clabo, shirtless and shoeless, adamantly denied any knowledge of the spotlighting of any deer.

"What's this, Mr. Clabo?" Halber inquired, pointing to Clabo's right knee. Clabo looked down and was horrified to see a rust-colored smear of fresh blood on his Levi's. "I've got the deer out in my truck," said Halber.

"I didn't shoot it," cried Clabo. "I admit I was there, but I didn't shoot it!"

Two down, one to go, thought Halber. But as it turned out, number three would be a long time in coming. Upon contacting Bradley Pane at his home, just before dawn, Halber found the man up and waiting for him. And he denied everything. It soon became apparent that a case against *this* man would depend solely on testimony against him by the other two—testimony Halber knew would never happen. Pane, too, knew it would never happen, and couldn't resist goading Halber.

"Looks like you're outta luck, Mr. Warden!" During the months that followed, Halber was not to forget these words.

It was the night before deer season the following year, long after Lysec and Clabo had paid the price for their misdeeds at Oregon Gulch. Halber was on night patrol near the old Cherokee Mine. Upon rounding a bend, he spotted a vehicle coming his way. For an instant, he clearly saw a spotlight being worked from the passenger side. But the light vanished immediately thereafter. Ten seconds later, Halber flipped on his red light and made a head-on stop of the oncoming vehicle. It was a dark-colored pickup.

Halber jumped out and hurried forward. He swept his flashlight over the open bed of the vehicle before illuminating its interior. A woman sat rigidly behind the wheel and a man occupied the passenger seat. Beneath the man's knees was a 12-volt, hand-held spotlight.

"Do you folks have any guns with you tonight?" Halber asked.

"No guns, officer. We're just out for a drive."

Halber asked the man to step out, and stand in the headlights. He then made a quick search of the cab for weapons. Nothing. But now he walked to the rear for a closer inspection. The pickup bed contained an impressive collection of car parts, some of which appeared to be hidden beneath a canvas tarp. Suspicious of the tarp, Halber approached warily, flashlight held high, his right hand on his gun.

With his left hand, still clutching the flashlight, he reached down, grabbed a corner of the tarp and whipped it back. And there, flat on his back, his face set in a grimace, his eyes tightly clenched, lay Bradley John Pane clutching a fully loaded .30-06 rifle.

"Well, well," said Halber, his memory flashing back to their last meeting. "Looks like you're outta luck, Mr. Pane!"

Tough Luck on the Little Sur

It was almost time.

Night had fallen, and the storm-tossed ocean pitched and rolled in the darkness. Heavy rain pelted down as the wind freshened, and the surf battering the Monterey County coastline boomed like cannon fire. Inland, in the rugged redwood canyons that drained to the sea, the streams began to rise.

The fish were there—bright, firm-bodied steelhead trout averaging better than nine pounds each. They milled around in a loose school just offshore, having gathered there during the preceding days and weeks.

Perhaps it was the rain that provided the change that set events in motion, or maybe the tide, or any of a dozen other more subtle things. Only the fish knew for sure. It was a 12-pound hen that reacted first, something having clicked in her brain. She started for the shallows, toward the giant rock that marked the mouth of Little Sur Creek. Unerringly she followed the sweet taste of salt-free water, a slave to the magic that had brought her back hundreds of miles to the stream where her life had begun. Others followed her, like sheep, and in seconds she and 40 more, dark missiles in the shallows, streaked across the tiny bar into the fresh-water lagoon beyond.

She had been three years in the ocean, dodging sharp-toothed predators, her life in constant danger. She had even suffered a narrow escape from the deadliest predator of all, and she still bore a reminder of the experience—an old fish hook lodged in her jaw.

But now, as she made her way up the seemingly peaceful waters of Little Sur Creek, she was soon to meet this super-predator again.

———————

They were poachers, steelhead snaggers, three of them. They trudged along, grim-faced, down the trail skirting Little Sur Creek. The stream had cleared and was back within its banks again, most effects of the storm two days earlier having vanished. A few paces behind the three outlaws, their captors followed—two uniformed game wardens. The wardens had charge of three drivers' licenses and three fishing outfits rigged with snag gear. The outlaws had ample reason for concern, for they had been caught fishing without fishing licenses, attempting to snag steelhead, and doing so in a stream closed to all fishing.

Two Fish and Game patrol vehicles were hidden among some trees along Highway 1. Upon arriving there, Warden Paul Maurer, using the hood of his four-wheel-drive pickup as a writing desk, began filling out citations. Lieutenant George Ritchie radioed for warrant checks on the men.

They were a good team, Ritchie and Maurer. Maurer maintained, as did all who knew the man, that George Ritchie, his supervisor, was certainly among the very finest wardens in the state. And Ritchie, had he been asked, would have said much the same about Maurer.

Ritchie was already beginning to regret the lieutenant's bars on his collar, resentful of the desk work that went with the promotion and robbed him of time in the field. He quite simply loved game warden work and firmly believed that it was perhaps the only profession in which you start at the top and work your way down.

"They're clear," said Ritchie, replacing the microphone on its holder.

"I told you so," said one of the poachers. "We're not criminals. We didn't know we couldn't fish here."

"Then why did you run?" Ritchie asked. Having no good answer for *this* question, the man simply shrugged.

They had indeed run, but it had come as no great surprise to the wardens. In fact the wardens had planned for it. The poachers had about them that nervous, fleet-footed look that wardens spot instantly. So Maurer had approached from upstream and had flushed the outlaws to Ritchie who was waiting in ambush on a narrow trail below. It had worked perfectly. When Ritchie, a six-foot, 200-pounder, stepped out in front of them, the lead runner stopped abruptly, causing a pile-up. Fortunately, there had been no injuries and no further resistance. With Ritchie writing one of the citations, the paperwork progressed swiftly.

The last violator had just signed his citation when the harsh, warning cry of a scrub jay sounded from an oak tree near the river. Both wardens turned for a look. They saw nothing at first, but then Maurer pointed to a willow thicket.

"Over there!" he said.

Ritchie had spotted them too, through the brush, a quick glimpse of several two-legged forms hurrying upstream.

"They must not have seen us," said Maurer.

"I guess not," said Ritchie. "I saw at least one fishing rod." The wardens then hurriedly finished their business with the first three poachers and sent them on their way.

"Good luck, men," said Maurer. "You're free to go."

They would *need* good luck, Ritchie thought to himself, for Judge Fowler, of the Monterey court, was not known for great sympathy toward steelhead snaggers. Only two weeks earlier, Ritchie had taken the judge and his wife on a hike along Little Sur Creek to acquaint him with the serious poaching problems the wardens were encountering there. It had been a worthwhile outing. The steelhead had been there, in numbers, sleek and beautiful, and Blue Rock Pool had been jammed with them.

Ritchie related to the judge how one well-known poacher in the area had recently employed a local technique known as "gaunching" and had yanked over a dozen large steelhead from Blue Rock Pool alone. The judge and his wife had been suitably outraged by the story. Ritchie knew then that it would go hard on the next poachers to get caught abusing the Little Sur steelhead.

So now, with the downtrodden trio of snaggers having departed, soon to test Judge Fowler's wrath, the wardens headed back to the stream to pursue the new bunch of outlaws just arrived.

It was slow going along the river. Through and around the willow and blackberry thickets they picked their way, avoiding the dense stands of leafless poison-oak, skirting boulders, and peering constantly ahead to avoid blundering onto the poachers and being seen. But it was a beautiful walk as well, even in winter.

Somewhere along the way a dipper, or water ouzel as they are sometimes known, joined company with them. Slate-colored, stub-tailed, resembling a large wren, it flitted about the stream from rock to rock, staying even with the wardens, dipping and bobbing and sounding its cheerful "zeet! ... zeet!" Its presence gladdened the hearts of the wardens, and as they watched, it dove into the water, swam down despite a stiff current, and took a stroll along the bottom, plucking a meal of insect larvae from the submerged rocks.

Amazing! thought Lt. Ritchie.

Poacher Ronald Guth, on a high rock overlooking Blue Rock Pool, took a final careful look around. He had come to considerable grief at the hands of wardens during his 33 years, and he had grown more careful. On this day, for instance, he had arranged for himself and his three companions to be dropped off at the river. There would be no parked vehicle on the highway to arouse suspicion. And he had taken into consideration what he believed to be the work schedules of the wardens in choosing this day.

Satisfied, he hurried down the steep bank to join his friends. Two of them had crossed to the north bank and were already casting to the dozen or so large steelhead clearly visible near the tail of the pool. A third man remained on the south bank with Guth. They used fly rods, with sinking lines and weighted flies. And while this would have seemed to many to be a crude way to snag fish, it was surprisingly effective. But Ron Guth, on this day, had another, far more effective, poaching method in mind.

From a willow tree, Guth selected a fairly straight branch about half the thickness of a broom handle. Using his belt knife, he quickly cut off the limb and trimmed it to about four feet. Then, from one pocket of his camo field jacket, he removed a large, long-shanked shark hook. Local poachers referred to them as "gaunch" hooks. Attached to the hook was a five-foot length of nylon cord with a loop in the end. With a few quick wraps of the cord, Guth lashed the hook to one end of the willow stick, then spiraled the remaining cord up the length of the stick to the other end. Slipping his hand through the loop in the cord and grasping the stick, he now had, in effect, a long-handled gaff—a highly illegal piece of equipment to possess on a steelhead stream. He next removed from another pocket a diving mask, also illegal on Little Sur Creek.

Thus equipped, Guth hurried to the upper end of Blue Rock Pool to a slab of granite that extended well out over the undercut bank. He pulled the dive mask down over his eyes, lay down on his stomach at the water's edge, ducked his head partially under, and peered down into the shadowy depths beneath the bank. He could see several large steelhead there, two within his reach, quietly stroking with their pectoral fins to hold their position near some exposed willow roots. The larger of the two fish within reach—Guth judged it to be about a 12-pound hen—had an old hook impaled in her jaw. With infinite care, Guth slipped the gaunch-hook device into the water and slowly . . . slowly moved the hook toward the 12-pound hen. Closer and closer the hook neared the fish, until the sharp point was poised directly beneath her belly.

But at this moment, Guth was distracted by the angry buzzing of a fly reel. One of his friends across the hole from him had snagged a fish. The fish, a nine-pounder, burst from the water, cartwheeled and landed with a great splash. It then rocketed upstream, where it nearly collided with Guth's target, the 12-pound hen with the hook in her jaw. The 12-pound hen, with a flip of her tail, shot farther back beneath the cut bank, out of Guth's reach. The snagged steelhead leaped again at the head of the pool, then raced downstream.

Guth again thrust his face into the water and peered beneath the overhang. Since the big hen was gone, he chose instead a slightly smaller male. Again he worked the gaunch hook toward the fish, ever so slowly, until the point was but a few inches below the fish's belly. Then, with a great jerk, he drove the barbed point deep into the fish's flesh.

The big fish exploded to the surface and thrashed wildly. The hook pulled free from the willow stick, which fell away, and Guth felt the nylon cord bite deep into his wrist. He rolled to his knees, grabbed the line with his free hand and yanked the big fish from the water, flinging it behind him into a bed of ferns. There it flopped and flailed until he grabbed a rock and ended its struggles with a sharp blow to the head.

Guth pushed the mask up on his forehead and gazed at the fish for a moment, recognizing it for what it was, a genuine thing of beauty. But he felt not one small twinge of regret. Instead, he pulled the hook from the fish's belly, recovered the willow stick and began rigging it again.

His friend across the pool had not dallied playing the foul-hooked fish, for sport had no place in their activities. Their stout snagging gear was heavy enough to horse in even a large fish, and so, after the foul-hooked fish's initial frantic and unstoppable runs, the snagger was able to haul it out with relative ease.

At this point, with less than six minutes of effort, the outlaws had scored two large fish. And Guth's companion on the south bank had hooked and lost a third. But it was then that their raid on the Little Sur came to an abrupt halt.

Guth had just returned to the granite slab and had pulled the mask down over his eyes again when he noticed his friends across the pool freeze and stare fearfully at something behind him. He spun around and gave a start as he met the cheerless gaze of a large game warden, 20 yards up the bank.

Guth's reaction was instantaneous. He flung away the gaunch rig, bolted past his startled companion and leaped into the thigh-deep water. This triggered a banzai charge on the part of the warden, and Guth's startled companion turned to find himself directly in the path of the charge. The man took one step back, dropped his rod and plopped down on his rump.

Guth, upon his initial jump into the stream, had lost his footing and plunged in, drenching himself. But he came up instantly and thrashed toward the opposite bank. The warden hesitated only a few seconds over Guth's now seated, still-startled companion. He plucked the man's wallet from his pants pocket, jammed it into a breast pocket of his own field jacket, and said with a thoroughly menacing look in his eyes, "You stay right here, and don't you move!" Guth's friend, wide-eyed with shock, nodded his head rapidly in understanding, prepared if necessary to sit there until spring.

Maurer now charged into the water and bulled his way across. As he emerged, he was surprised to see that his quarry had chosen to flee straight up the mountainside which rose steeply from the north bank of the stream. It was a puzzling choice of escape routes, but Maurer could only follow. As he climbed, a long stone's throw behind Guth the gaunch man, he was aware that the two snaggers from the north bank were also in full flight, but heading in a more logical direction.

George will get 'em, thought Maurer with certainty.

Rocks dislodged by Guth now rained down the slope, and Maurer had to dodge them. Then all at once an outcropping gave way under Guth's weight. He frantically grabbed another rock, and it too gave way. Losing his balance, he fell backwards, arms flailing, and began rolling down the mountainside. Maurer, seeing him coming, wisely stepped aside as the man tumbled past, part of a small avalanche.

But 15 feet on down the slope, Guth checked his fall and managed to regain his footing. There was an instant of eye contact between him and the warden, then he was off again, scrambling away to escape. But Maurer didn't hesitate. He took two running steps down the slope and launched himself. One hundred eighty-five pounds of game warden knocked Guth flat from behind, and the two men then tumbled together down the remaining slope, wiping out a stand of poison-oak, cutting a swath through a thicket of blackberries and plunging into Blue Rock Pool with a resounding splash.

Lieutenant George Ritchie, having witnessed Maurer's remarkable descent down the mountainside, regretfully abandoned his pursuit of the remaining two poachers and rushed to the aid of his friend. Guth had come up fighting, swinging, twisting and jerking violently and emitting loud, guttural grunts. Maurer had him from behind, in knee-deep water, but it was all he could do to hang on. Then Ritchie arrived. Guth spotted Richie and instantly stopped fighting, simply going limp.

"Oh, George," he said. "It's you!"

Again using the hood of his patrol truck to write on, Warden Paul Maurer scratched out a citation for Guth's friend, the remaining snagger. He had earlier returned the man's wallet, albeit a bit damp, and placed the two steelhead and the gaunch hook in the back of the truck.

"What about me?" said Ronald Guth, steelhead gauncher, his hands cuffed securely behind his back.

"You're gonna have to go with me, Ron," said Lt. Ritchie. "I told you if you ever ran from us again I'd take you to jail."

The warning had been over a year earlier, but Guth remembered.

"I can't believe my bad luck," said Guth, looking at Ritchie and shaking his head. "You're supposed to be on your day off!"

"Yes," agreed Ritchie, reminded of Judge Fowler and his outraged wife. "Definitely tough luck!"

A mere week following her return to the Little Sur, the big hen steelhead again passed through the freshwater lagoon on her way back to the ocean. But she no longer weighed 12 pounds, the natural process of spawning having reduced her weight considerably. Beneath the great rock at the mouth of the stream, she passed again over the bar, and for the second time left behind the stream where she had spent the first year of her life. She was spent and tired, and the rusty hook in her jaw troubled her, but she had beaten the odds and completed the cycle. If her luck continued she would return in a year to spawn again.

Upon reaching the breakers, her body immediately began to reverse the wondrous changes that had allowed her to survive in fresh water. But she would linger awhile near the mouth of the stream to lessen the shock and regain her strength. The bottom shoaled away sharply here, and dark forests of kelp grew nearby.

She never really saw the bull sea lion that got her, just a bright flash of ocher the instant before his jaws crushed the life out of her. And in the feast that followed, another sea lion joined in, and within seconds there was nothing at all left of the big fish, no sign that she had ever lived.

Except for in the clear waters of Little Sur Creek, in the clean gravel bottom of a wide riffle above Blue Rock Pool . . . where a tiny spark of life glowed in each of several thousand tiny, gem-like eggs.

The cycle had already begun anew.

SERIAL POACHER

SISKIYOU COUNTY, CALIFORNIA

The eagles were first to catch the warden's eye—three of them, fierce-eyed golden eagles, dark against new-fallen snow. They paused from their meal as the distant patrol vehicle left the road and headed their way. Then a flurry of powerful wing beats launched them skyward.

Warden Rennie Cleland, California Department of Fish and Game, had long ago learned to pay attention to eagles. For many times over the years they had alerted him to the work of game poachers. And it was to the pursuit of game poachers and related outlaws that Cleland had dedicated his life.

He drove to the spot where two headless carcasses lay in the snow. Tight-jawed, he stepped from his vehicle to glean what he could from the bloody scene. Both animals were mule deer bucks, well into the rut, at least 180 pounds each. The heads of both had been hacked off just below their chins. *Why?* Cleland wondered. The much-valued gray, winter-thick capes had been left to rot.

There was little to go on. No tracks, no clues. Cleland could only photograph the scene and drive away. But he would alert the ranchers, the sheriff's deputies, the power company linemen, all who could act as eyes and ears for him in the weeks to follow—all who could alert him to the presence of anyone who didn't belong.

When the patrol vehicle had grown small in the distance, the eagles warily circled lower, then glided in to land.

———

It was a brittle-cold evening, two weeks later, just before dark. Deputy Andy Herbst, Siskiyou County Sheriff's Office, spotted a suspicious-looking pickup near Juniper Lodge. It sat unoccupied, half-hidden amid high bitterbrush near Highway 97. Herbst and Richard Coots, U.S. Forest Service, parked out of sight and awaited whoever might return to the pickup.

It was pitch dark when the dome light of the pickup suddenly came on. Two men had returned. But in the few seconds it took Herbst and Coots to approach them, the men were able to stash two high-powered rifles behind the seat. They claimed they had been unarmed and had simply been out for a "nature walk." Herbst and Coots, in frustration, could only fill out field identification cards on the two and release them.

Later, Warden Rennie Cleland examined the cards. One of the suspects, Clayton J. Sorgatz, age 40, of Klamath Falls, Oregon, was a man he would later have reason to recall.

———

Twelve months passed. Warden Cleland was again working the Juniper Lodge area, the prime winter-range country where the poaching had occurred the year before. Upon discovering fresh tracks on a little-used dirt road leading east off the highway, Cleland drove in to investigate. At once his suspicions were aroused.

Shallow, ice-covered puddles in the road had not been disturbed. Someone had intentionally driven around them. A quarter mile from the highway, near a gate into the McMillan Ranch, the tracks left the road and continued out through the bitterbrush and junipers. Following the faint trail with his eyes, Cleland spotted a white pickup hidden in the trees.

As quietly as possible, Cleland backed back down the road and hid his patrol vehicle. He then slipped out with his radio, binoculars and flashlight, and crept back toward the hidden pickup. When certain no one was around, he approached the vehicle and peered through a window.

There was no visible evidence of firearms, but on the floor, in front of the passenger seat, lay an Oregon deer tag. Straining his vision to the utmost, he read the name printed on the tag: Clayton J. Sorgatz. His pulse quickened. Reaching for his radio, he called Deputy Andy Herbst.

"You'd better roll this way," he said, then went on to explain the situation.

Visible in the snow, a single set of lug-soled boot tracks led southwest from the pickup. Cleland waited for sunset, then began following the tracks. He knew immediately his quarry was hunting. It was clear to see from the tracks. The man had taken short steps, seeking out the quiet ground, pausing often.

The trail looped around to the east, through patchy snow along a hillside, through scattered junipers and pines. But it was largely open country—dangerous country for the task at hand. Cleland remembered with clarity being warned by a deputy that a well-known local outlaw had boasted of once having had Cleland's badge squarely in the cross-hairs of his rifle scope.

Seeing no advantage for continuing, Cleland chose a spot in the shadows and settled down to wait. It was nearly dark when movement caught his eye. A man wearing a black and white plaid coat strode into view a mere 30 yards away. Cleland let him pass, noting a scoped rifle slung over his right shoulder and a pair of binoculars around his neck.

When he was nearly out of sight in the gathering darkness, Cleland silently fell in behind him. The man angled down from the high ground to a shortcut across an open stubble field at the edge of the valley. Cleland shadowed him, keeping him just barely visible ahead. Cleland now whispered frequently into his radio, keeping Herbst advised.

"Why don't you drive in to McMillan's gate," said Cleland. "I want to see this guy's reaction. Then you can turn around and drive back out again."

Andy Herbst soon complied, and at the first sight of approaching headlights, the man sprinted toward the tree line. There he dropped to one knee under a pine, hiding until the headlights had departed. He then hurried the short remaining distance to the white pickup. With Herbst waiting out on the highway, Cleland decided to stay out of sight and allow the man, still ignorant of his peril, to drive on out. *We'll see what he tells Andy,* Cleland thought.

By the time Cleland made it to his patrol vehicle and out onto the highway, the white pickup was already stopped a half mile to the north, bathed in the red and blue glare of Deputy Herbst's emergency lights. The man, still in his black and white plaid coat, was standing between the two vehicles with Herbst studying his driver's license. The scoped rifle was lying across the hood of the patrol car.

"Mr. Sorgatz here claims he was just out for a nature walk," said Herbst, as Cleland approached. "Says he didn't have his rifle with him."

"I *saw* you with a rifle," said Cleland, looking the man over. He was a lean six-footer, with dark hair and remarkably cold, dark eyes.

"I didn't have a rifle," Sorgatz insisted. "But even if I did, I have the right to bear arms!" He was growing agitated, and both officers sensed instability in the man.

Cleland ordered Sorgatz to face away and gave him a quick pat-down search. No weapons, but from the right front pocket of his jeans, Cleland withdrew four shiny brass .22-250 cartridges.

"You need these on a nature walk?" said Cleland. Sorgatz made no reply.

Sorgatz adamantly denied he had been hunting, but Cleland, unmoved, issued him a citation for hunting without a non-resident license. Sorgatz reluctantly signed in the box and was allowed to leave, but he did so without his custom made .22-250 rifle, the four cartridges, his binoculars and a pair of Buck hunting knives. These Cleland had seized into evidence.

The following day, Cleland returned to the McMillan Ranch. There, he backtracked Sorgatz's trail a half mile or so to an uprooted pine tree at the edge of a cultivated field. It was obviously Sorgatz's stand. Close at hand on either side were heavily used deer trails leading from the sparse forest to the harvested fields and to the alfalfa haystacks beyond. It was a perfect place to poach a buck.

Later in the day, Cleland checked with McMillan and determined that Sorgatz had no permission to hunt on the ranch. The man was also guilty of hunter trespass. Cleland swung by the district attorney's office and amended Sorgatz's citation to include *this* charge as well. He then began preparation for the jury trial that he was dead certain would follow.

At his arraignment, Sorgatz pled not guilty, requesting a public defender and a jury trial.

LAKE COUNTY, OREGON —SIX WEEKS LATER

It was a yearling doe, winter-tame, a mere 50 yards from the road. Don and Betty Williams, on an outing in their Bronco, spotted her on a hillside a good quarter-mile ahead. She browsed, unconcerned, amid the sage and bitterbrush. The Williams also noticed as brake lights appeared on the rear of a white pickup they had been overtaking. The driver had apparently seen the animal too and was stopped in the gravel roadway to look at it.

The driver was so intent on the deer that he failed to notice the arrival of the Williams as they pulled to a stop a few yards behind him. He appeared to be fumbling for something on the seat to his right.

Being in no hurry, the Williams waited patiently for the driver to continue on. Then they were alarmed to see him suddenly thrust a rifle barrel out the window and take aim at the doe. They were horrified as the rifle boomed and the doe crumpled and fell.

The Williams sat stunned for a moment, unsure of what to do. Then Betty came to her senses, grabbed a pen and jotted down the man's license number, just as the pickup door flew open. The man stepped out, and when he spotted the Williams, their unexpected presence struck him like a physical blow. He recoiled a step, a crazed, cornered animal look in his eyes. This frightened Don Williams, who stomped on the gas sending gravel flying as the Bronco leapt forward. It swerved around the doe killer and his pickup and went careening away down the road.

The following day, Don Williams, still frightened, phoned Oregon State Police.

Trooper Scott Moore, Oregon State Police, Wildlife Division, listened intently to the caller. Scribbling notes, he asked a few questions, verified a license number and got a clarification on a location. Then he headed out the door. This was just the call he'd been waiting for. Gunshot deer had been showing up all over the winter range, and now, finally, he had a genuine lead to go on.

En route from Lakeview, to the remote valley south of Adel, Moore radioed in the white pickup's license number. It came back to one Clayton John Sorgatz out of Klamath Falls. A cell-phone call to Sergeant Glenn Smith in the Klamath Falls office soon verified that Clayton Sorgatz was still a resident there and still owned the white Ford pickup. Sergeant Smith also advised Moore of Sorgatz's recent arrest in California.

"Rennie Cleland says he's a bad one," said Smith.

The directions were good, and Moore had no trouble finding the dead doe. But he could find no shell casings on the road, only a cigarette butt of unusual brand which he slipped into a labeled envelope. He then loaded the doe into his pickup and headed back to Lakeview. On the basis of the Williams' observations alone, he could *easily* get a search warrant for Sorgatz's residence.

Mid-afternoon the following day, three Oregon State Police units and a U.S. Fish and Wildlife Service vehicle pulled into Sorgatz's lair in Klamath Falls. They were armed with not only a search warrant, but an arrest warrant as well. Within minutes

Sorgatz found himself handcuffed and seatbelted into a patrol car as officers swarmed through his house and outbuildings. When questioned, he admitted to being in the area south of Adel, but claimed he had been hunting only coyotes. He adamantly denied killing the doe.

The searching officers immediately began to find incriminating evidence. In short order they recovered seven sets of fresh mule deer antlers taken long after the close of deer season and 75 packages of frozen venison.

From his white pickup they seized an expensive, bull-barreled .22-250 rifle equipped with a 4 to 12 power variable scope with range finder and bullet-drop compensator. From the ashtray of the same vehicle they recovered a California resident hunting license in Sorgatz's name. It had been purchased on the same day, six weeks earlier, that he had tangled with Warden Rennie Cleland, for hunting *without* one.

When the search was completed, Sorgatz was given what the state troopers considered a long-overdue, one-way ride to Lake County Jail. He would face charges in both Klamath and Lake counties, plus the charges still pending against him in California.

———————

The trials of Clayton Sorgatz, one in California and two in Oregon, occurred in the spring, within three weeks of each other. The Oregon proceedings were slam-dunk, the evidence overwhelming. There was even a bullet-to-rifle match of a .22-250 slug, miraculously intact, dug from the carcass of the doe whose killing had been witnessed by the Mr. and Mrs. Williams.

In California, however, it was another story. Rennie Cleland had charged Sorgatz with yet another charge, that of making a fraudulent statement to obtain the California resident hunting license. This was in reference to the license recovered at his home by the Oregon state troopers, a license he had attempted to present in court on the date of his arraignment. But these charges, Sorgatz knew, could possibly be beaten, particularly through a jury trial.

After all, there was no evidence that he had actually *killed* anything in California. Warden Rennie Cleland, who understood these things better than most, prepared himself for a long, hard fight.

But in the end, on the verge of his trial, Sorgatz's resolve crumbled. Perhaps it was the arrival of three Oregon state troopers, spit-shined and inspection-perfect in their dress blues and Smokey Bear hats. Sorgatz knew that the testimony of these men could hurt him in a variety of ways. But for whatever reason, he gave up, settling for a plea bargain.

When it was all over, the sum of Clayton Sorgatz's sentences in both California and Oregon amounted to roughly $4,000 in fines and two years' probation with no hunting. Plus, he lost his two custom-made rifles valued at well over $1,200 each. While not a huge penalty, in view of his crimes, it was certainly enough to deter any normal person from such destructive practice. But then, there was nothing *normal* about Clayton Sorgatz.

―――――――

Shortly following his convictions, Clayton Sorgatz vanished from southern Oregon. But where had he gone? The wardens and troopers who knew him pondered this question with a certain uneasiness. For the crimes of outlaws of Sorgatz's rare type, those who kill often, without remorse, simply to see things die are a bit frightening. When and where would he kill again? Time alone would tell.

THE COLLECTORS

Queenie the strike dog winded it first, the smell of death on the morning air. Trotting down a logging spur, sniffing the ground, with Elmer Dade's pickup rattling along close behind, she suddenly stopped, threw her nose skyward and bristled. Elmer hit the brakes, killed the engine and stepped out. Following Queenie, he strode a few yards and peered down into a small ravine.

"Queenie, get back!" he shouted. The dog instantly backed away.

Elmer cursed under his breath then began to count, ". . . four . . . five . . . six . . . seven . . . ." There were at least eight of them—eight skinned and crudely butchered carcasses of poacher-killed deer. Dade's first impression was that he had stumbled onto the illegal bait pile of some outlaw bear hunter, but it was in the wrong place for a bait pile.

No, thought Elmer Dade. *This is the work of some real serious deer poachers.*

An hour later, Dade pulled into a mini-mart and phoned CalTIP.

It was late afternoon when Warden Bob Pirtle, California Department of Fish and Game, followed a good set of directions to the small ravine. Like Elmer Dade, Pirtle's first reaction was anger, for this was evidence of poaching on a grand scale.

He stood there for a while, studying the smelly tangle of partially fleshed skeletons and hides. What could they tell him? For starters, he noted that the remains were in varying stages of decomposition. While some of the bones were picked almost clean and had begun to bleach, obviously weeks old, others appeared fresh, with red meat still attached. *An ongoing thing,* he thought.

Turning his attention now to the hides, Pirtle found bullet holes in some of them, often poorly placed holes. Looking closer at the pink and bloody flesh side of one of the freshest of the hides, he noticed bits of straw adhering to it. *Probably skinned in a barn somewhere.*

He next examined the short lengths of distinctive orange baling twine tied to the hind legs of each deer. The deer had obviously been hung for skinning by means of this twine. Using his pocket knife, the warden bent down and cut off a piece of the twine for later reference.

Before leaving the site, he photographed the grisly pile, aware of the impact the photo would have on some future jury should he get lucky. And with so little to go on, he knew he would have to get *real* lucky.

Back in his patrol truck, Pirtle located the dump site on a Forest Service map. It was well within the El Dorado National Forest, but he noticed that not far away were a scattering of mile-square sections of private land as well, many of them totally surrounded by National Forest. An examination of the various roads near the site told him little, but it gave him an idea.

Early the next morning, Pirtle phoned Mike Power, Special Agent for the U.S. Forest Service. Power had been around a long time and knew the National Forest, and the people who lived and worked in or near it, as well as anyone Pirtle knew. Following greetings and small talk, Pirtle got down to business. He described what he had found at the dump site and gave Power its precise location.

"The way I figure it," said Pirtle, "whoever's doing this must live close, probably within a couple of miles. And it looks like the deer were skinned in a livestock barn. Do you have any ideas?"

Power pondered the question, and Pirtle could hear the crinkling of paper as the man consulted a map.

"Well, I see two possibilities," said Power. "There's a convicted pot grower who lives near there. He's on searchable probation, so we could search him any time. And there's another bunch who live out on Rock Creek Road. I was there once and talked to a guy named Spradlin. The sheriff's office had received complaints of fully automatic weapons fire near his place, and I went there to investigate. Spradlin was carrying a shotgun the whole time I was there. Wouldn't put it down. He's a real strange fellow, probably a dope grower. They've built an outbuilding there that actually sits on National Forest property, so we've got a good excuse to go there and discuss it with them. Of these two possibilities, I would lean toward the latter."

"Maybe we should pay 'em a visit," said Pirtle.

———————

Dark clouds were spitting snow as the short procession of three patrol vehicles ground its way up the steep and heavily switchbacked Whaler Creek Road. Special Agent Mike Power and a sheriff's deputy were in the lead vehicle, followed by Bob Pirtle and Warden Ken Ball. Bringing up the rear was Warden John Dymek. Pirtle had called Dymek and Ball for help, and he had suggested they bring rifles. Ordinarily, two or three wardens would have been plenty for such a task, which was at best a shot in the dark. But the reports of automatic weapons were worrisome.

Jack Spradlin's lair was an unsightly blight on what would otherwise have been a scenic mountain meadow. It was as though the four-room shack, the tiny barn and the chicken coop had been thrown up amid a relocated half acre of the county dump. But the house had doors and windows, and it was through one of these that

Marjorie Stubbs, Spradlin's girlfriend, spotted the approaching patrol vehicles.

As Special Agent Power, in his Forest Service pickup, pulled up near the front door, Dymek and Ball drove their vehicles wide to either side. As per their plan, Pirtle and Powers jumped out and headed straight for the front door. Dymek and Ball remained behind their vehicles, Ball covering the house while Dymek guarded the barn and chicken coop. Each man was armed with a Mini-14 assault rifle, loaded and ready for instant use. But they kept these weapons out of sight.

When Pirtle and Power were halfway to the front door, Ball spotted a curtain move, then a face at one window. The face instantly vanished, and Ball heard rapid footsteps on a wooden floor.

"Someone's running through the house!" he shouted.

Pirtle was first to arrive at the front entrance, ready for anything. Stepping slightly to one side of the door, he knocked loudly. As he awaited a response, his eyes were drawn to a series of ragged, pencil-diameter holes, belly-high across the wooden door. Puzzled at first, it suddenly dawned on him with a shock. He was looking at bullet holes—bullet holes from a weapon fired from inside the house.

Oh, God, I'm dead, he thought, looking for a place to dive. But at this moment, instead of gunfire, the door creaked open a few inches, and Pirtle got his first look at Marjorie Stubbs.

Marjorie Stubbs appeared to be about 40. In fact, she was 28. With stringy, mouse-colored hair and a drawn, rodent-like face, she would never have been pretty, but aside from her lack of beauty she had that haggard, hard-used look common among drug people. And Pirtle had no doubts but that this was exactly what she was. But she would never be accused of a lack of devotion to Jack Spradlin, for tattooed in bold black letters across the knuckles of each of her hands, one letter per knuckle, was the name JACK.

That must have melted his heart, thought Pirtle.

"What do you want?" demanded Marjorie Stubbs.

"We'd like to talk to you about a few things," said Pirtle. "Is Mr. Spradlin here?"

"No, he's not," she said, slipping out through the door. As she did so, when the door opened wider, Pirtle glimpsed a large crimson and black banner on a wall across the room.

Is that what I think it is? Pirtle asked himself. But Marjorie quickly closed the door behind her.

Pirtle now launched into a series of questions about Spradlin's whereabouts and his expected time of return. But Marjorie Stubbs professed total ignorance concerning Spradlin.

"And, of course, I'm gonna need to hear about the deer," said Pirtle, and from the change in Marjorie's eyes, he knew instantly that he'd come to the right house.

It was about then that the door behind Marjorie's back decided to slowly swing open again on its own accord. Both Pirtle and Power gawked at what they saw within, for in addition to a large Nazi war banner, black swastika and all, there were racks of exotic-looking weapons, including a German MP-40 light machine gun. Marjorie quickly turned and pulled the door closed again.

"Is that a machine gun you have in there?" Pirtle asked.

"It's not really a machine gun anymore," Marjorie stammered. "The barrel's plugged."

In the meantime, Warden Dymek had joined the deputy sheriff, who had beckoned him to look at something near the chicken coop.

"Look at this," he said, pointing to a rust-red smear in the dirt. "And this," picking up a piece of fresh bone.

As Dymek studied what was obviously blood and probably deer bone, the deputy approached the chicken coop, a three-walled structure open on the back. Arriving at the open rear of the structure, he gave a low whistle and called again for Dymek. Dymek walked over and was treated to the sight of a skinned and partially butchered deer, hanging by orange baling twine from a main roof support of the chicken coop. Dymek did an about-face and hurried off to advise Pirtle.

Pirtle, through further questioning of Marjorie Stubbs, had just determined that there was another woman in the cabin when Dymek arrived with the news of the deer. Leaving Marjorie Stubbs with Power, Pirtle called Dymek and Ball together for a quick conference.

"We need to go for a warrant," said Pirtle. "We have great probable cause to look for more deer meat in the house. If you guys stay here and secure the place, I'll go for the warrant. I can probably be back by early afternoon."

"I agree," said Dymek. "But I think we should do a quick walk-through now for officer safety. Spradlin may be hidin' out in there somewhere with another machine gun."

All agreed that this was a good idea. So Pirtle, backed by Dymek, again approached the bullet-riddled front door.

"What are you gonna do?" asked Marjorie Stubbs. "You can't go in there."

"We're just gonna do a quick search of your house for people," said Pirtle. "Just people, nothing else."

Despite Marjorie's protests, Pirtle now carefully pushed the door open. Remaining as concealed as possible, he peeked in.

"I don't believe this," he said under his breath.

By far the least astonishing thing he saw inside was a young woman, holding a baby and sitting near a wood stove. For all around her was what could only be described as an arsenal. There were racks of guns and Nazi war banners on every wall, and beneath these were stacks of cases of ammunition. It was with difficulty that Pirtle forced his attention back to the woman.

"State officers, ma'am," Pirtle announced. "We're gonna have to ask you to step outside, please. You'd better bring a coat, it's real cold out here."

The woman sullenly complied, bundling the baby in a blanket. Pirtle and Dymek then drew their sidearms and headed into what was not only an arsenal, but a museum of the Third Reich. From room to room they slipped along, covering each other, marveling at what they saw. They searched everywhere a man could hide.

More guns. Guns and ammunition everywhere. Crimson and black banners with swastikas everywhere.

There were several bench-mounted reloading presses with 25-pound kegs of gunpowder at hand and cases of primers and bullets. In one back room, Pirtle was startled to encounter a camo-clad man in a Nazi helmet poised in a corner. Pirtle ducked, raised his pistol, then lowered it again when he realized he was facing a mannequin. Dymek checked a shower stall, unused in recent history, and discovered a fully loaded MAC-10 submachine gun equipped with a silencer. There were tables and work benches strewn with tools, gun parts, silencer parts, and a case of what looked like grenades.

But it was in the last room that they encountered a sight that stopped them cold, like a slap in the face. It was simply a doll. But it was a doll obviously representing a non-Aryan child, and it hung by a rope from the ceiling, a hangman's noose tight around its tiny neck.

On their way out, their walk-through completed, the grim-faced wardens paused briefly to examine a large hole hacked through the living room floor. A pit lay beneath it, roughly six feet deep and wide enough to easily accommodate at least a half dozen people. A half dozen fighters, to be more exact, for it was obvious that the pit was intended to shelter defenders should the place ever come under siege.

Outside again, Pirtle briefed Ken Ball and the others on what he and Dymek had observed inside. Agent Power immediately made a cell-phone call to his boss, Steve Morgan, Agent In Charge in the area. Morgan would soon prove himself a genuine man of action. Pirtle then discussed the situation with the others and they made decisions, including what to do about the two women and the baby.

Their plans made, they approached Marjorie Stubbs, who suddenly found herself under arrest on the deer and gun charges. She was handcuffed and soon headed for town with Power and the deputy sheriff. As for the younger woman, who Marjorie Stubbs claimed was only visiting, the wardens identified her to their satisfaction, then allowed her to leave with the baby.

"Looks like you guys will be on your own for a while," said Pirtle, addressing Dymek and Ball. For they alone were to remain to guard the house.

Pirtle climbed into his patrol truck, and as he was pulling away, he called out the window, "Keep your eyes open, guys. We're dealin' with some real spooky folks here." Then he was off, down the driveway and out of sight.

It was snowing again, and now the snow was beginning to stick. Dymek and Ball turned up their collars to the cold and settled down to wait.

"I was talkin' to that deputy," said Ball, "and he said he thinks these people have ties with Hells Angels . . . That they may even cook dope for' em."

"I don't doubt it," said Dymek. "But I do know that they were cookin' a lot of what looked like stew in there. Probably venison stew. There were big pots of it on a wood stove, and there were smaller containers covered with foil, like they were gonna take it some place . . . like they were gonna feed a lot of people."

The more the wardens mulled these thoughts over in their minds, the more nervous they became, half expecting at any time to hear the ominous rumble of approaching Harleys.

It was when they had been at the Spradlin place about three hours, awaiting Pirtle's return, that Ken Ball decided to pay the chicken coop a visit and have a look at the evidence deer. He was just approaching the open rear of the structure when suddenly he was startled and amazed to see a human form erupt from a pile of straw and chicken manure.

Jack Spradlin had been caught by surprise when the law arrived. Engaged in butchering the deer, he had assumed the approaching vehicles were those of his friends. By the time he discovered his mistake, it was too late for him to make it back to the house or flee into the forest. Nor could he make a stand and shoot it out, for he had left his MAC-10 submachine gun in the house. His only option was to hide. So, he had burrowed into the straw pile where he had remained motionless, evading detection until he could no longer stand the cold. But now, freshly emerged, he stood shivering, teeth chattering, face to face with a surprised, but very competent-looking game warden.

"Put your hands up!" demanded Warden Ball, crouched at the ready, his hand on his gun butt.

Ball had to repeat the command before Spradlin's cold-numbed brain responded and he complied. Dymek now came dashing up, and he, too, was amazed at the sight of Spradlin, who stood filthy, smeared to the elbows with deer blood, his wild, hippie-length hair festooned with bits of straw and chicken droppings.

Too cold to complain, Spradlin was immediately handcuffed, searched, and stuffed into the passenger seat of Dymek's patrol truck. Dymek fired the engine, turned the heater on high, and left Spradlin, seatbelted in, his legs secured with a bad-boy strap, to hopefully thaw out enough to eventually speak.

Hours passed. It was nearly 3:00 p.m. when the sounds of approaching vehicles set Dymek and Ball to nervously fingering their rifles. But it was Pirtle with the signed search warrant. He was closely followed by an entourage of support vehicles arranged for by Agent In Charge Morgan. First came a SWAT team van, from which leaped five evil-looking, flak-jacketed, armed-to-the-teeth commando types. They immediately took up positions around the perimeter of the property to act as guards.

Next came a sedan bearing an agent from Alcohol, Tobacco and Firearms. Morgan had known that ATF would be highly interested in the machine guns. Following ATF was a couple of El Dorado County Sheriff's units with deputies to assist in the search. Then came a U-Haul truck in which to transport the expected large volume of evidence. Bringing up the rear was a truck loaded with a diesel generator and tower-mounted, high-intensity flood lights. Morgan had correctly predicted the search would continue until long after dark.

In fact, the search lasted until about 3 o'clock the following morning. Fish and Game remained the lead agency, and Pirtle served as the official "finder" of the hundreds of items of evidence.

It began slowly at first, the searchers simply wandering around the house gawking. But then they settled down to business, and Pirtle was hard-pressed to keep up with logging and describing each piece of evidence.

It became clear soon after the search began that Spradlin and company were much more than simply collectors. They were suppliers as well. Not only were there a number of fully automatic weapons, but there was considerable evidence indicating that Spradlin functioned as a gunsmith, specializing in the conversion of semi-automatic weapons to fully automatic. There were large numbers of conversion kits, mainly for converting AR-15 rifles to fully automatic. And there was considerable evidence that large amounts of ammunition were being loaded there, and that booby trap components were being manufactured there from smoke grenade parts.

Searching an assigned part of one room, Dymek found several "broom handle" machine pistols, and he was fascinated by display cases containing Nazi SS things, including uniform items, medals and ceremonial daggers. Propped in a corner, near a window, he found a fully loaded World War I German sniper rifle with a telescope sight nearly as long as the barrel. It was a beautiful piece, but deadly.

They could have capped us at half a mile with this, he thought.

Continuing with the search, Dymek started through a chest of drawers in one bedroom. In the top drawer, wrapped in a bloody T-shirt, he was surprised to find a large chunk of fresh deer meat. He showed it to Pirtle. "She must have been cutting this up for stew meat when we arrived," said Pirtle.

Searching further in the chest of drawers, Dymek found a photo album. Paging through it, he noted photos and a newspaper article concerning Spradlin's arrest two years earlier for pot growing in Mendocino County. Then there were more recent photos taken in pot gardens elsewhere. The photos often showed various individuals, armed with automatic weapons, posed with freshly killed deer against a luxuriant backdrop of eight-foot-tall marijuana plants. Dymek studied the deer in the photos. Several were bucks still in velvet.

Obviously killed well before deer season, he thought.

Shortly before dark, a pickup pulled into the driveway, its driver apparently puzzled over the commotion. The earlier snow had now turned to rain, and while the various officers visible outside the house were in rain gear, the assortment of official vehicles was in plain sight. Despite this fact, Joseph Bentley, certainly a candidate for "dumb crook of the year," decided to linger and make inquiries concerning his friend, Jack Spradlin. He soon found himself surrounded by cops, relieved of a loaded .32 revolver in his jacket pocket, and under arrest for carrying a concealed weapon. And as if this weren't enough, a sharp-eyed deputy recognized him as one of the machine gun-toting pot growers in the photo album. It was off to jail for Joseph Bentley.

A very wet night descended on the scene, and all present mentally thanked Morgan for his foresight. The generator was fired up, the outside floodlights brought to bear, and smaller lights were strung to illuminate the inside of the house. For the Spradlin place lacked both power and running water.

The search continued, with a constant procession of officers carrying thoroughly described, logged and photographed items of evidence to add to the growing pile in the waiting U-Haul truck.

"Does anyone know what a LAWS rocket is?"

All heads turned toward the ATF agent, a young man obviously new to the job. Dymek examined the object of the question. Sure enough, it was a rocket launcher of the type capable of instantly reducing a small building or vehicle to wreckage.

The next surprise came when a Forest Service agent, searching a wrecked camper in the yard, discovered a satchel of plastic explosive. *What next?* the searchers wondered. What was next turned out to be a clear plastic bag containing several ounces of white powder that field-tested positive for methamphetamine.

But the rest of the night produced only more of the same–more weapons, more Nazi stuff, more evidence of the curious worship of a regime that had once plunged the world into a war that had killed over 30 million people.

Pirtle pondered these thoughts near the end of the search as the other officers from the various agencies finished their work, packed their gear and started back to Placerville. Then Pirtle, too, took one last look around, climbed into his pickup and headed out. Behind him in the darkness, the Spradlin place lay gutted and silent.

———

The trial of Jack Spradlin was in its fourth day, and things were not going well for the prosecution. The defense, it seemed, was successfully convincing the jury that Spradlin had had nothing to do with the machine guns, the dope, and the other contraband. It was their contention that it was Marjorie Stubbs who was the machine gun-collecting, bomb-making, drug-cooking, Nazi-worshiping villainess. Spradlin's attorney was claiming that his client didn't even know of the existence of any of the illegal things found in the house.

The prosecution was now desperate for some way to directly implicate Spradlin. Pirtle, after hours of pondering the problem, decided to again examine the photos in the album Dymek had found. Upon studying them again, he fixed his attention on a single photo. It was the shot of Joseph Bentley, machine gun in hand, kneeling beside the dead deer in the marijuana garden. But there was a second person in the photo, behind and off to one side of Bentley. This person was holding a distinctive-looking, camouflaged and scoped M-16 assault rifle, a fully automatic weapon that had been seized during the search of Spradlin's residence.

But unfortunately, the photo had captured this second person only from about the shoulders down. There was no face to identify. But, on closer observation, Pirtle noticed a tattoo on the man's left forearm. Using magnification, Pirtle identified the tattooed image as that of a cobra in a threatening pose.

Afraid to get his hopes up, Pirtle phoned the county jail. Upon reaching a jailer, he first verified that Jack Spradlin was still in custody there. He then asked a favor.

"I need to know if he has a tattoo on his left forearm, and if so, what it is."

"No problem," said the jailer. "Hold on." Two minutes later the jailer was back. "Yeah, he has a tattoo, a big cobra."

———————

It was but a day or two later that Jack Spradlin again had reason to contemplate his tattoo. Shackled and manacled, en route to Vacaville in a van with barred windows, he stared at his forearm, studying the colorful image of the snake. Twenty years earlier, it had cost him $40 and an hour of mild pain. Now it would cost him six years in state prison.

ABOUT THE AUTHOR

Author Terry Hodges is a retired Fish and Game patrol lieutenant. For most of his 30-year career, he supervised the wardens in two Northern California counties. Unlike most warden supervisors, he was a field man, leading his wardens from the front, doing hardcore warden work until the day he retired. He was also a pilot and spent hundreds of hours flying single-engine planes, mostly at night, directing his wardens to violators he spotted from the air.

As a vastly experienced, 30-year veteran game warden, Terry writes with a special understanding of his colorful and often dangerous profession. The stories compiled in his books are considered by many to be the best of their kind, and readers come away with a vivid picture of what the lives of game wardens and conservation officers are really like.

Terry has received national writing awards and was three times chosen Writer of the Year by the *Outdoor Writers Association of California* (OWAC). In addition to his seven books, he has been a regular contributor to the Department of Fish and Game's magazine, *OUTDOOR CALIFORNIA*. He served four years in the U.S. Coast Guard and received his Bachelor of Science degree from California State University at Sacramento.

In 2006, Terry was inducted into the *California Outdoor Hall of Fame*.

THE
WARDEN FORCE
SERIES

All titles available in print, eBook, and audiobook format.
Visit **WardenForce.com** for more info and previews.

NIGHT RIDER: SEASON 1

The Midnight Ride of Bonnie and Clyde: Wardens tangle with a murderous mother-and-son poaching team.

Night Rider: A California warden pursues highly dangerous night-poachers of wild pigs.

Decisions: Wardens off the coast of Southern California's Catalina Island risk their lives to save the crew of a sinking commercial squid-fishing boat.

A Second Second Chance: A California game warden ambushes outlaw catfish fishermen using baby swallows for bait.

The Collectors: California wardens take on a nest of Nazi-worshiping, weapons-collecting, deer poaching outlaws.

Nothin' Personal: California wardens track down a thief who steals the head and antlers of another hunter's buck.

Bottom Feeders: California wardens go after a band of white-trash, sturgeon-poaching hillbillies with attitudes.

An Outing with Team Taylor: A California game warden and his family, on a short vacation, team up to capture antelope, bear and steelhead poachers.

Rookie: A rookie California game warden gets his first taste of his hazardous new career.

Grand Trickery: A California warden employs a magnificent bluff to catch outlaws night-poaching deer.

Tough Luck on the Little Sur: California wardens pursue gaunch-hook steelhead poachers.

Serial Poacher: Wardens pursue a disturbing and dangerous lone-wolf deer poacher.

The Vision: A boy's fondest dream comes true.

GRIM WITNESS: SEASON 2

A Matter of Little Choice: Wardens hunt down an exceptionally large and highly dangerous wounded mountain lion.

The Meaning of Pursuit: Fleeing felons and a wild, white-knuckle ride for a reserve game warden.

Gambler's Luck: A big-rig load of alfalfa holds a surprise hidden in a chamber among the bales.

The Departure of Bully's Luck: A cruel bully gets what he deserves.

Pollard on the Rock: An alert clerk at a one-hour photo shop sends wardens in search of outlaw houndsmen.

Fools and Small Victories: A warden targets a particularly destructive brand of violator.

Renegades: Wardens target a destructive pair of elk poachers.

Bear Crazy: A warden investigates the poaching of an exceptionally huge bear, killed with a broadhead arrow at a garbage dump.

A Message Delivered: Wardens hunt down antler thieves.

Sting: Wardens close in on a band of abalone poachers.

Cave Man: California wardens tangle with a wild-looking, hairy, commercial crab fisherman from Oregon.

Skinny Bob: California wardens go undercover to capture commercial reptile rustlers.

Grim Witness: Dangerous pot-growing poachers use pipe bombs to kill king salmon.

DELTA GHOSTS: SEASON 3

Delta Ghosts: A team of wardens ambush outlaw gillnetters at Grizzly Bay, in the same Delta waters patrolled 80 years earlier by Fish Patrol warden and famous writer, Jack London.

Smooth Operator: Wardens stalk a cagy and arrogant abalone-poaching commercial sea urchin diver.

Time Bomb: A dangerous and mentally unstable deer poacher proves highly troubling for pursuing wardens.

Cheaters: An inexperienced warden consults an old pro of his profession to capture a pair of super-wary striped bass snaggers.

Tiger's Revenge: A cocky and confident salmon poacher makes the mistake of "pulling the tail of the tiger;" that is, taunting a local game warden.

A Calculated Risk: Despite a comedy of errors, wardens close in on highly destructive pig poachers.

Killer John: Future serial killer? Wardens deal with a scary deer poacher and born killer.

New Talent: A new warden astounds a mentor with his almost super-human sensory skills.

Slow Learners: A one-time major league pitcher proves to be a highly interesting adversary for wardens.

Davie Crockett and the Bush Baby: A Hollywood stunt man and elk poacher tangles with border wardens.

Then Came Speedy: A Peruvian sheepherder and a small sheepdog pay dearly to save their sheep from marauding bears in high meadows of the Sierra Nevada range.

Lethal Intent: Would-be assassins are thwarted by a fearless warden who puts his life on the line for the intended victims.

COLD, COLD HEARTS: SEASON 1

Trash Can Joe: Wardens pursue an infamous, outlaw hunting-guide who uses donuts to illegally bait bears. Meet "The Black Robinhood."

Callous Hearts: A rogue band of meth-cooking deer poachers meets with misfortune.

Rascal's Road to Justice: "The world's greatest duck caller," as a renowned waterfowl violator bills himself, crows that he's too smart to be caught. His education to the contrary soon follows.

True Remorse: One of the coldest of the cold, cold hearts, pays a heavy price for extreme cruelty to a trapped bear.

Turkeys: The wardens meet a hardened criminal whose hobbies are turkey hunting and home-invasion robberies.

A Weekend with "Starsky and Hutch": A swashbuckling pair of wardens cram a fourth-story, roof-to-roof foot chase in old San

Francisco and heroic rescues from burning buildings into a single, memorable weekend.

The Natural: A young woman proves that she was born to be a Fish and Game warden.

Dirty Harry and Ape Island: A warden thinks his way out of a jam in this story that features a good-humored Highway Patrol sergeant and an ill-humored monkey.

Lucky Breaks: A warden demonstrates his substantial tracking skills to put away an outlaw houndsman who traffics in bear gallbladders.

Lobster Jake: An infamous lobster pirate teams with "The Muppet," a character straight out of a nightmare.

Cold, Cold Hearts: A California warden, at great risk to himself, flies to Alaska to help state troopers there deal with a team of highly dangerous, cruel and destructive grizzly poachers.

Delta Ambush: Season 5

Uncatchable 'Chick' Feathers: A clever deer-poaching archer, widely considered to be too smart to catch, meets an old-time game warden who disagrees.

Incident at Killer Cove: Armed killers on the run tangle with game wardens on the prowl.

Sooner or Later: An outlaw falconer outsmarts a new and inexperienced game warden. A year later, he's not so lucky.

Otter Killers and Uncommon Luck: Wardens pursue sea-otter-killing commercial abalone divers.

Leo's Demise: One man dies before wardens deal with an African lion, a grown pet gone rogue, in the suburbs of Los Angeles.

Tough Customers: A game warden and a hostage-taking armed robber nearly destroy a drugstore.

Bug Pirates: Trap-raiding lobster thieves meet with misfortune.

Setliners: Wardens target long-line catfish poachers.

A Matter of Preference: Wardens attempting to ambush season-jumping commercial lobster fishermen get a big surprise.

Delta Ambush: Night-prowling, canoe-borne wardens stalk a wily and destructive Delta outlaw.

Rake Man: A well disguised warden outsmarts lawless abalone pickers.

The Honest-to-God Truth: An honest mistake and a white-knuckle, midnight vehicle tail through Long Beach yields a surprise and an important arrest.

Raid of the Stockton Airborne: Did they or didn't they? Wardens from the sky? A day for mass-killing duck poachers does not end well.

ORDEAL AT SKULL CANYON: SEASON 6

Scum of the Delta: A lone warden faces three armed and dangerous outlaws at night on a lonely Delta island.

Night of the Beach Walkers: Wardens set a trap for renegade abalone pickers on an island off the California coast.

The High Cost of Greed: A massive overlimit of snow geese equals bad news for greedy poachers.

The Best Medicine: A young boy provides a cure for racial tension.

Ordeal at Skull Canyon: A dark night and a mistake on an offshore island nearly proves fatal for a young warden.

Hoffman's Lucky Shot: A lucky break spares the evil life of a dangerous poacher.

Moseley's Reward: A well timed tip sets wardens on the trail of outlaw mountain lion trappers.

Herpie and the Snake Lady: Wardens raid an absolute house of horrors and target lawless reptile dealers.

Road Hunter: A road-hunting pheasant poacher leads a clever warden to pull off the most spectacular arrest of his career.

Harold's Toughest Race: A tough, marathon-running warden amazes everyone by running down an escaping would-be rapist.

Fatal Flaw: One dark mountain night, a lone warden, at great personal risk, bluffs a lawless band of brush-cutters to arrest a deer poacher and a wanted felon.

Tuffy's Sweet Moment: An epic foot chase ends in near death for a fleeing violator.

An Ending of Sorts: A warden-turned-writer, one winter's evening, reflects on his career and that of his long-dead mentor.

DEADLY INTENT: SEASON 7

Skin-Head Fred: Wardens tangle with a murderous, meth-cooking, game-killing Neo-Nazi.

Spreaders: Wardens target a highly intelligent, super-wary commercial lobster pirate.

Deadly Intent: An alert warden stays alive and saves a life.

The Poor Eyesight of Love: The arrest of a man and wife poaching team reminds wardens that love can indeed be blind.

Ruthless: Crossbow-wielding, night-hunting outlaws face sly wardens who never give up.

Ghost of the Feather: Salmon poachers on the Feather River mix it up with an old pro warden.

Abalone Boy: An abalone-poaching commercial sea urchin diver earns his way into state prison.

Anything but Cheap: A tough young warden targets ruthless, bear-killing houndsmen.

Knock-and-Talks: A highly experienced, slick-talking warden outsmarts goose and deer poachers.

Woody Peckerwood: A dumb crook story in which the dumb crook steals the wrong man's boots.

Kegger: Wardens break up a midnight keg party, and a gutsy college student becomes an instant legend.

The Troubling Case of Walter Sumpter: A highly troubled teenager commits a terrifying crime with ominous implications.

MASTERS OF DESTRUCTION: SEASON 8

A Matter of Survival: A warden's worst fear nearly comes true.

Some Kind of No Good: A warden's exceptional skill and some blind luck combine for an interesting outcome.

Payback Time: The vengeful victim of a childhood bully retaliates years later, his revenge spectacular.

Drop-Countin' at Gunner's Swamp: A long-retired warden helps two employed wardens make an important duck overlimit case.

Threats and Promises: A search warrant search of the home of two deer poachers yields surprises, plus a brush with a bad cop.

An Extra Set of Eyes: An aging game warden lieutenant, a few days following knee surgery, ends up being far more than an observer during the action-packed, nighttime arrest of salmon poachers.

Operation High Hog: A large team of wardens pit their wits against some of the worst deer and pig poachers in California history.

Primal Instincts: Wardens pursue the puzzling case of two deer poachers who kill far more deer than they could ever use.

Combat Fishing: An old warden, his days of foot-chases far behind him, employs stealth and trickery to capture two fleet-footed young salmon poachers.

Masters of Destruction: A fearless and horribly destructive ATV-riding deer poacher repeatedly evades wardens and officers of other agencies before finally going down hard.

The Ghosts of Tipper Slough: A wealthy farmer pays far more than money when he ignores a warden and destroys a particularly wonderful wetland.

Leonard's Bad Word: Does a warden known for never using profanity have a slip-up over his radio one dark night?

Trophy Poacher: A disturbing, physically imposing, trophy-hunting poacher and a monster wildfire put wardens to the test.

THE WORST OF THE WORST: SEASON 9

Not Bad for a Fish Cop: A lone warden, during two consecutive nights, outsmarts two criminals and makes two unrelated felony arrests.

Fuzz-Face, Snake Eyes and Fu Manchu: The unscrupulous camp host of a high-mountain campground employs three bow-hunting criminals to take out a camp-raiding dumpster bear.

Repeat Offenders: An aging warden recounts his long history of capturing the same salmon and deer poachers time after time.

Swift Justice: Fleeing salmon poachers run afoul of poisonous plants and relentless wardens.

The Worst of the Worst: Determined wardens spend months bringing down a band of smart, super-wary deer poachers, among the worst in California history.

Masters of Deception: A husband and wife poaching team prove to be unskilled game-law violators and even worse liars.

Trouble in Hog Heaven: The cruel and unscrupulous operators of a big-money pig-hunting club are targeted by determined wardens.

The Cycle: Wardens outsmart a well-organized team of abalone poachers.

The Caviar Connection: A team of undercover wardens stalk a ring of sturgeon-poaching caviar dealers.

The Old Pro: A crafty old warden, a master of his trade, dazzles a much younger warden by outsmarting and capturing two hardened deer poachers.

Zero Choice: A lone warden, nearly gunned down by a fugitive dope grower, reassesses his approach to his hazardous occupation.

Death on Snake Mountain: A warden performs a nerve-jangling search of a mountain home said to contain dozens of free-roaming rattlesnakes and a two-week-dead human body.

Confession: A young warden nearly kills a man and keeps a secret for over 30 years.

Heartless Bastard: A warden comes out second best when he tangles with a man with no legs.

COMING SOON

The *Warden Force* prequel

Featuring Legendary Game Warden
Gene Mercer